ALSO BY DAN LACY

The Meaning of the American Revolution
The White Use of Blacks in America
The Birth of America
The Lost Colony
The Colony of Virginia
The Lewis and Clark Expedition
The Colony of North Carolina

THE ABOLITIONISTS

★—by—★

Dan Lacy

McGRAW-HILL BOOK COMPANY
New York St. Louis San Francisco Düsseldorf London
Mexico Sydney Toronto

Book design by Kathy Peck.

1 2 3 4 5 6 7 8 9 0 B P B P 7 8 3 2 1 0 9 8

Library of Congress Cataloging in Publication Data

Lacy, Dan Mabry, date
The abolitionists.
SUMMARY: Discusses the efforts of those men and women who worked toward the total abolition of slavery in the decades before the Civil War.
1. Abolitionists. 2. Slavery in the United States —Anti-slavery movements. [1. Abolitionists. 2. Slavery in the United States—Anti-slavery movements].
I. Title.
E449.L117 322.4'4'0973 77–26872
ISBN 0–07–035753–6

CONTENTS

FOREWORD

DURING the decades before the Civil War, the "abolitionists," those dedicated men and women who wrote and spoke and petitioned for the immediate and total abolition of slavery, were resented and feared, even hated, not only in the slaveholding states but in the free states of the North as well. They were regarded as unreasonable and fanatical disturbers of the national peace of mind.

When the Civil War brought the end of slavery they had so long fought for, abolitionists enjoyed a brief time of acceptance and respect. But they wanted more than a legal end to slavery; they wanted true equality between blacks and whites, in education, in voting, in job opportunities, in human dignity. And this not even the Northerners, who had defeated the Confederacy and freed the slaves, were yet ready to give. Most black freedmen were forced to continue working the farms and plantations of the South under a system that gave them little more than slavery did. Their right to vote was guaranteed by a new amendment to the Constitution, but the opportunity to vote was taken away by fraud and violence. Education open to blacks was limited and meager, and black students were almost always barred from white schools and colleges. By 1900 most of the opportunities and rights hoped for, other than the end of slavery, had not been achieved. The abolitionists became an almost forgotten part of what seemed to be a lost struggle.

Respectable white leaders, north as well as south, accepted this outcome. But the heirs of the abolitionists did not. Many of the children or grandchildren of pre-Civil War abolitionists banded together with others, black and white, to form the National Association for the Advancement of Colored People in 1909. They fought hard for the restoration of Negro rights and little by little made some progress, until in 1954 they won the great Supreme Court decision declaring the segregation of blacks in schools to be unconstitutional. Soon laws were enacted and court decisions handed down which demanded black voting rights, equal opportunities for employment, and the end of segregation in all public places. These newly asserted—or reasserted—rights took a major and often bloody struggle. There was a true revival of the spirit, the courage, the total dedication of the old abolitionists. Men and women, blacks and whites, youths and elders, from north and south, risked their lives in the early 1960s to win freedom at last. This time the abolitionist drive succeeded where it had faltered after the Civil War. Anything like full equality in housing, income levels, and other aspects of life is still far away for most blacks, as it is for Indians, Hispanic immigrants, and even poor white Americans. But at least the legal fights have been won. And the abolitionist spirit lingers to press on with the remaining issues.

This struggle of our own time has made us realize how great a debt we all owe to those original abolitionists—the zealous, dedicated, even fanatical men and women, white and black, of more than a century ago. This book is an effort to recall them to memory for today's young Americans of all races.

Many people have helped with this book, but I want to express my very special gratitude to Walter Green who edited the manuscript and with great skill and a thorough knowledge of the subject made a major contribution to the work.

DAN LACY

★ I ★

The FIRST FOES of SLAVERY

WHEN the United States declared its independence from Britain on July 4, 1776, and proclaimed that all men are created equal and have the right to life, liberty, and the pursuit of happiness, hundreds of thousands of black Americans did not share in this freedom. They were slaves: bought, sold, owned, and worked like horses or cattle their whole lives through. Though they had been ready to rebel against Britain over the slightest threats to their own freedom, few white Americans saw anything wrong with slavery or wanted to take action to end it.

Slavery existed in every one of the thirteen colonies that had declared themselves independent. Though some Indians were slaves, most of the slaves were black men, women, and children. They or their parents or ancestors had been seized in Africa and brought to the New World. The few slaves who ended up in the North usually worked as house servants. But in Maryland, Virginia, the Carolinas, and Georgia slaves made up a large part of the population and were essential to the economic life of those states. The South's agriculture and industry—the production and export of tobacco, rice, indigo, and "naval stores" (tar, pitch, rosin and turpentine)—depended heavily on slave labor.

Most white people, in the North and in the South, including many who disliked slavery, thought that blacks were childlike and unintelligent and could not manage for themselves if they were free. In fact, though, many thousands of free Negroes—blacks who had been set free or bought their freedom—were managing quite well for themselves, in spite of great prejudice against them.

Of the small number of white men and women in the Colonial period who were troubled about slavery, many were members of the Society of Friends, or Quakers, as they were called. The Quakers were peaceful folk who had settled in Pennsylvania and Rhode Island and whose religion taught them that all people are equal in God's eyes. Not all Quakers followed this belief and some even owned slaves. The cooks and maids and butlers and coachmen of the wealthy Quaker merchants of Philadelphia often were blacks who had been bought or inherited. But even the slaveowners among the Quakers treated their enslaved servants kindly.

One Quaker for whom kindness was not enough was Benjamin Lay, a small man with a misshapen back who stalked the streets of Philadelphia denouncing slavery and attacking slaveowners in bitter and unQuakerly language. Once he interrupted the quiet of a Quaker meeting by waving a sword, which to the Quakers was an instrument of evil. He condemned those who claimed to live by the Golden Rule and yet enslaved others. "It would be as justifiable in the sight of the Almighty, who beholds and respects all nations and colours of men with equal regard," he shouted, "if you should thrust a sword through their hearts as I do through this book!" And with that he stabbed a Bible with his sword. Hidden inside the book was a container of red dye that looked like human blood. It gushed out, spattering those around with what Lay called the stain of their guilt for tolerating slavery.

Lay shocked the quiet and dignified Quakers, but a gentle man named John Woolman, carrying the same antislavery message, moved them deeply. Woolman was born in 1720 to a Quaker family in New Jersey. His first contact with slavery came as a young man. Woolman had a little knowledge of law and added to his income by drawing up legal documents. His employer, who wanted to sell a black house servant, asked him to write a bill of sale. Woolman knew and liked the woman who was to be sold. He felt he must do as his employer told him, but he was horrified to have any part in the selling of another human being. Never again, as long as he lived, would he draw a will or bill of sale or any other document that recognized slavery. He became convinced that slavery must be done away with, abolished.

Woolman became a successful storekeeper; but when he found that business took up too much of his time, he sold his store and supported his family as a tailor. He had been present at Benjamin Lay's outburst in the Quaker meeting, a scene that stayed vividly in his mind, as did an antislavery pamphlet Lay had written.

When he was twenty-six years old Woolman went with a Quaker friend on a walking trip to North Carolina, during which he saw slavery on a large scale on the plantations. After his return he wrote out his thoughts in an essay entitled *Some Considerations on the Keeping of Negroes,* which the Quakers published in 1754. Gently but firmly, Woolman pointed out that slavery went against Christian ideals. "To consider mankind otherwise than brethren," he wrote, "indicates a lack of understanding of God's universal love and makes one less Christian."

Woolman made another trip to the South, again on foot, in 1757, and in 1762 published a new edition of his essay. It received wide circulation and eventually did much to persuade the Quakers to ban slaveholding by their members.

Woolman's views were shared by Anthony Benezet, a well-educated French Huguenot who made his home in Philadelphia and became a Quaker. Like Woolman's, his heart went out to the slaves. He worked quietly in the Quaker community and opened and taught a school for blacks.

Woolman's and Benezet's ideas gradually won acceptance among Quakers. The Philadelphia Yearly Meeting of the Society of Friends agreed in 1758 that no member who bought or sold slaves could attend its business meetings. Though they opposed buying and selling, the Quakers were slower to insist that members of the Society free the slaves they already owned or might inherit. But by 1788 Quakers throughout America were required to free their slaves, including even those in the states of Maryland and Virginia, where slaves were important to the farming economy.

Though opposition to slavery in Colonial and Revolutionary America was strongest among Quakers, there were others who shared their views. In 1773 Benjamin Rush, a Philadelphia doctor, published *An Address to the Inhabitants of the British Settlements in America, upon Slavekeeping.* In it he attacked slavery as strongly as had Woolman. He argued as a scientist against the popular idea that blacks were inferior humans who should be kept as slaves for their own good. To those who claimed the Bible recognized slavery, he pointed out that every ideal of Christianity opposed it. If the Bible had upheld slavery, said Rush, that would be a reason to disbelieve the Bible.

A growing number of Puritans in New England were coming to share the Quaker view of slavery. One of them, Samuel Hopkins of Rhode Island, in

1776 published *A Dialog, Concerning the Slavery of Africans.* Hopkins bitterly attacked the racial prejudice that made slavery possible. How were reasonable men able even to think of allowing slavery? he asked. "Our education has filled us with strong prejudices against Blacks, and led us to consider them, not as our brethren, or any degree on a level with us; but as quite another species of animals, made only to serve us and our children; and as happy in bondage, as in any other state."

The coming of the Revolution led many more Americans to think about slavery. How could they claim freedom for themselves as a natural right of all men while they kept others in slavery? Many leaders of the Revolution like Benjamin Franklin and Ezra Stiles opposed it, as did some slaveholders like Thomas Jefferson and George Washington, who later freed his own slaves. Throughout the new states of the North emancipation laws were passed, beginning with Vermont in 1777. In Massachusetts the courts declared that slavery was automatically ended by the state's Bill of Rights. By 1804 every state north of Maryland had provided for the freeing of all slaves, either immediately or gradually over a period of time. In 1787 the Northwest Ordinance provided that there should be no slavery in the territories west of the Appalachians and north of the Ohio River—what are now the states of Ohio, Indiana, Illinois, Michigan, and Wisconsin. Even in the southern states slavery was no longer as profitable as it once was, since the Revolution had cut off naval stores. A few manumission societies were formed in Maryland, Virginia, and North Carolina to urge the freeing of slaves.

But when delegates gathered in 1787 to draw up a new Constitution for the United States, it was clear that the southern states would belong to no union and accept no Constitution that did not recognize and protect the right of the individual states to maintain slavery if they chose to do so. The most that could be gained was a provision that after 1807 Congress would be free to bar the bringing of additional slaves into the United States.

When that year came, Congress did in fact vote to forbid the further importation of slaves. But it did so less because of an opposition to slavery than because of a dislike and fear of persons with black skins. Northerners who wanted no part of slavery and had freed the few slaves in their midst feared that if slavery were ended, thousands of free blacks might come up from the South. White workers feared they would compete for jobs. Property owners feared they would become criminals and rob and steal. Others worried that they would become dependent on charity.

White Southerners had an even greater fear of free blacks. They might put ideas of freedom in the minds of slaves. They might slip into the slave quarters of plantations at night and stir up slaves to run away or even to rise up and kill their masters. (And with good reason, for free blacks like Gabriel Prosser did form plots to fight for freedom.)

The fear of free blacks thus discouraged any movement to emancipate slaves. Many whites thought an answer would be to send free slaves back to Africa or elsewhere to which free Negroes could be sent. In 1817 the American Society for Colonizing the Free People of Color of the United States was organized. It was to be known generally as the American Colonization Society. Some very distinguished men, all Southerners and slaveholders, joined in founding it, including George Washington's nephew, Bushrod Washington, John Randolph, and Henry Clay. The purpose of the organization was "to promote and execute a plan for colonizing (with their consent) the free people of color, residing in our country, in Africa, or such other place as Congress shall deem most expedient." The place chosen was Liberia, in western Africa.

Some who supported colonization claimed that it would help to end slavery by providing a place out of the country for slaveowners to send the blacks they freed. But it was *free* Negroes those who favored colonization wanted to be rid of, not slaves or slavery. If large numbers of slaves had been freed, there would have been no adequate shipping to send them in and almost no money to pay the costs. Nor were more than a handful of free blacks ever willing even to think of moving to Africa. America had become their country.

At the end of America's first fifty years of independence, nowhere was there any large, organized movement demanding the end of slavery.

★II★

BENJAMIN LUNDY and the BEGINNINGS of the ABOLITION MOVEMENT

BY 1808 slavery was no longer a national institution. It existed only in the five original southern colonies—Maryland, Virginia, the Carolinas, Georgia—and their westward extensions in Kentucky and Tennessee. It seemed to be weakening in Virginia and Maryland, where tobacco growing was not making enough money to meet the cost of caring for slaves. In the upper south, manumission societies were working to persuade owners to free their slaves.

Well into the 1820s many Americans let themselves think slavery was a dying institution that would disappear if left alone. An American Convention for Promoting the Abolition of Slavery which had been formed in 1794 to bring together local manumission societies faded out of existence as interest waned. But the development of cotton as the great American crop and the opening of new slave territory in the West made slavery again a powerful and growing menace.

Except for a special kind of "sea island" cotton that could grow only along the Carolina and Georgia coast, the seeds of the cotton plant were very difficult to separate from the surrounding fibers. The labor time spent in cleaning seeds from the cotton was more than the crop was worth.

In 1793 Eli Whitney, a Yankee, as Northerners were known, saw the problem while visiting a southern plantation. He invented a clever and inexpensive device called a cotton gin that could tear the seed from the fiber swiftly and cheaply. Even more important, during the same generation British inventors had created machines that could spin and weave cotton by water power or later by steam. Mills were built that could pour out cloth endlessly. This created a nearly unlimited demand for cotton. The cultivation of cotton and the need for labor to grow it increased tremendously.

The invention of the steamboat in 1807 made it easy to travel up the Mississippi and other rivers and opened hundreds of thousands of fertile acres to cotton planters. People spilled west into upland Georgia, western Tennessee, the new states of Alabama and Mississippi.

Suddenly, farmers in the South could become rich by raising cotton. But they needed laborers to clear the fields and plant, cultivate, and pick the cotton.

The price of slaves doubled and tripled. Even in states in which cotton could not be successfully grown, such as Virginia and Maryland, a great deal of money could be made by selling the newly valuable slaves to planters in the cotton states.

In New England as well as in Great Britain a thriving cotton goods industry was created. The wealthy manufacturers and bankers of that region, eager for abundant supplies of cotton, approved of the system of slave labor that made it available. The export of cotton to Great Britain earned the money that paid for the imports needed to build America's cities and open the West. Cotton was king in the economic life of the whole country, not just the South.

Southerners no longer thought of the death of slavery. Now they demanded its expansion. Settlers were spilling over beyond the Mississippi into the vast Louisiana Purchase territory acquired from France in 1803. Should this new land be slave or free? By 1819 the question could not be ignored, for Missouri was asking to be admitted to the Union as a slave state. It would give the nation eleven slave states and only ten free states. And it would open the way for allowing slavery in all the western territory across the Mississippi.

After a bitter, angry debate, Congress reached an agreement: the Missouri Compromise. Missouri was admitted as a slave state, but Maine was admitted at the same time as a free state to keep the balance. The southern boundary of Missouri, extended to the west, was to be the boundary between free and slave states as they might be created in the future from the Louisiana Purchase.

But thoughtful men knew that the agreement would not last permanently. Former President Thomas Jefferson said the struggle over Missouri's admission came "like a fire bell in the night," and that the Compromise was "a reprieve only, not the final sentence." John Quincy Adams, then secretary of state, noted that it was "a mere preamble—a title page to a great tragic volume." It was clear that slavery, left to itself, would expand across the West.

The opposition to slavery began to organize and grow stronger. Benjamin Lundy became the first nationally known spokesman of that opposition. As were so many early antislavery leaders, he was a Quaker. He was brought up in New Jersey, near John Woolman's home, and absorbed the ideas Woolman planted in the Quaker communities there. In 1809, at the age of twenty, Lundy left home and joined the westward movement to the Ohio Valley. He settled first at Wheeling, on the Ohio River, in what is now West Virginia but was then part of Virginia, where he became an apprentice to a saddle maker.

The newly opened plantations along the lower Mississippi were booming and hungry for slaves. Thousands of blacks no longer needed in Virginia were being sold south to meet this demand. Often, the slaves were driven like cattle across the dusty Virginia mountains to Wheeling, where they were loaded on boats bound for plantations in Mississippi or Louisiana. Lundy later spoke of his horror at seeing "ragged men, chained together and driven through the streets, *bare-headed* and *bare-footed, in mud and snow,* by the remorseless SOUL SELLERS, with horsewhips and bludgeons in their hands." His experience in Wheeling led Lundy to devote the rest of his life to a struggle against slavery.

By this time he was twenty-six. Lundy, now a married man and an experienced leather worker, had settled in the free state of Ohio. He opened a saddle and harness shop, and began his work against slavery. In January 1816 he had a broadside (a one-page announcement) printed and distributed in the neighboring towns and villages. In it he said he had "resolved, and fully determined" never to lay down the antislavery cause "while I breathe, or until the end be attained." He called on his neighbors to found an organization to oppose slavery, and hoped it would grow to include everyone in the country who shared its views.

Soon, Lundy and a few of his neighbors set up the Union Humane Society, devoted to ending slavery, opposing racial prejudice, and helping the free blacks in Ohio. Though the society attracted several hundred members, there was little they could actually do. They had no means of spreading their ideas or of limiting slavery. The members lost interest and the organization melted away.

The next few years were frustrating ones for Lundy. He moved his business to Missouri, which was about to be admitted as a state. Congress had voted not to forbid slavery in Missouri, and Lundy wanted to be there to help elect antislavery delegates to the convention that would draw up the state's Constitution. Most of Missouri's settlers had come from the South, however, and the proslavery forces won overwhelmingly.

Lundy returned to Ohio, almost wiped out financially. In 1820 he abandoned his harness business and started an antislavery newspaper, which he called *The Genius of Universal Emancipation.* Issues came out irregularly because most of the money to print the paper and support Lundy's family had to come from subscriptions, and sometimes Lundy was forced to take on saddle-making jobs to live. He had to turn from one printer to another, because some printers were afraid to be involved with a publication that angered so many people. Sometimes Lundy would have to have the paper printed in Steubenville, Ohio, and then walk back home carrying the entire issue on his back.

He moved again the next year, to Tennessee, a slave state, when a small antislavery organization, the Tennessee Manumission Society, offered him its printing press to publish his newspaper. But he soon became convinced that he could be much more effective working in a large eastern city than in the Tennessee mountain village where he lived. He decided on Baltimore, Maryland, for he felt that he should still work in a slave state where he would have a better chance to reach the slaveholders themselves.

In 1824 Lundy set out alone from Tennessee to walk the hundreds of miles to Baltimore. He went a roundabout way, along mountain paths and dusty roads into North Carolina, visiting Quaker settlements there, and then on through Virginia, seeing slavery at first hand as he went. As soon as he reached Baltimore, he started his newspaper again, but now he had a much wider national audience. As soon as he had enough money he sent for his family.

Most abolitionists before Lundy and those who were to follow him called slavery sinful. Lundy, too, believed it was sinful, but he saw that a peaceful end to slavery could come only if the southern states voted to do away with it. And he did not believe that southern voters could be persuaded to do this by calling them sinners. He tried instead to convince them that slavery was unprofitable and that black farm laborers would produce far more as free men working for wages than as slaves. But the trouble was that no matter how slavery impoverished the white farmers who had to compete with the slaves, no matter how it retarded the growth of cities and industries in the South, it was quite profitable for the slaveowners themselves. And they were the ones who controlled the governments of the southern states.

Nevertheless, Lundy patiently explored practical ways to end slavery. He proposed that Congress abolish slavery immediately wherever it had the power, as in the District of Columbia and the territories, and use its constitutional authority over interstate commerce to forbid the sale or transportation of slaves from one state to another. He urged the southern states to provide that every slave born after a certain date would be free when he or she became an adult. He thought about what would happen to the newly freed blacks if slavery were indeed ended, and decided that the American Colonization Society was doing a useful thing in giving them help if they wanted to leave the country. But he never agreed that blacks should *have* to leave as a condition of their being freed. Instead he thought that freed Negroes should be given an education and land or other economic aid. With this preparation they should be allowed to live anywhere in the United States they chose, and should have all the rights that whites have. This would require northern states as well as southern states to change many laws that discriminated against blacks. Lundy knew his program would take a long time, depending as it did on the willingness of the southern states to abolish slavery voluntarily. But he was willing to be patient. Slavery was a sin, and he was sure that God in his time would end it.

In 1826 Lundy went to Haiti to try to persuade the new black republic to pay the expenses of freed Negroes who wanted to settle there. He had no success, and the trip took much longer than he had planned. He sailed back to Baltimore to find that his wife had died in childbirth, leaving newborn twins. Lundy never remarried, and his children were placed with friends and relatives. The rest of his life he spent traveling or living in rooming houses or with friends. Only near the end did he attempt to make another home.

He began to abandon hope that southern slaveowners could be reached either by moral or economic arguments. Southerners were angrily attacking even the most moderate questioning of slavery. The only way to be rid of slavery, Lundy concluded, was to elect officials who would repeal the laws protecting it and would require its abolition. In 1827 he organized the Maryland Anti-Slavery Society, the first organization pledged to political action to end slavery.

Though Lundy's efforts had often met with ridicule or anger, he had never been in physical danger. But now proslavery feelings were growing stronger. In January 1827, Austin Woolfolk, a Baltimore slave trader, met Lundy in the street, knocked him down, and beat him nearly senseless. When the case came to trial, the judge accused Lundy of having provoked the slave trader.

Lundy became so discouraged about the South that he began to look to the North to organize anti-slavery support. In Boston in 1828, speaking to some young liberal ministers and reformers, Lundy was tired, seedy, and unimpressive. Yet one listener, a thin, red-haired, balding man in his early twenties, was more excited than he had ever been in his life. His name was William Lloyd Garrison.

Garrison had been apprenticed to a printer. He had became an editor as well, helping with the publication of a Boston newspaper dedicated to reform. He wanted to make the world better. All sorts of ideas boiled up within this young man. Somehow he saw the love and strength with which Lundy had spent his life on behalf of the slaves. He attached himself to Lundy, following him, eager to learn from him. For Lundy it was wonderful to see so much admiration in the eyes of a follower.

In the summer of 1829 Garrison came to Baltimore. Lundy's newspaper, *The Genius of Universal Emancipation,* was reborn. It had been intended as a monthly, but with Garrison came new hope and new resources, and the paper became a weekly. With Garrison able to edit the paper, write editorials, and set type, Lundy had time to travel, study slave conditions in the South, write reports, and organize support. Though Lundy and Garrison differed in many ways, they worked well together and the paper became an important power in the antislavery movement.

But Garrison's bold attacks on the slave trade soon got him into trouble, and he landed in jail for six months after writing that a shipowner whose vessel had been used to carry slaves from Baltimore to New Orleans was like a highway robber and murderer.

When he was released from jail, Garrison returned to Boston. Without his vigor *The Genius of Universal Emancipation* failed again financially. In 1831 Lundy moved to Washington, hoping to resume publication there.

Throughout the United States controversy over blacks was growing more bitter. Southerners were now defending slavery not as a necessary evil but as a positive good. Many Northerners as well became very hostile to blacks. There were riots in

Cincinnati and other cities in which the homes and businesses of free Negroes were burned. Laws against free Negroes were passed in many northern states, forbidding them to own property or to vote or even to settle in the state.

Lundy became discouraged about ending race prejudice in the United States, so that blacks and whites could live as equals. His interest in colonization rose again, not as a way of getting rid of free Negroes, but as a way of giving them a better chance. He went to Ontario, Canada, in 1832, and found that the severe winters, hostility of many Canadian whites, poverty of the black settlers, and quarreling among themselves made Canada much less than a paradise for blacks, though it offered them more freedom than did the northern states.

Returning to the United States, Lundy sought money for a vast new scheme. Texas was still part of Mexico. The laws of Mexico did not permit slavery. Here was an enormous free territory, close at hand. The climate was perfect for growing cotton and other crops with which black workers were familiar. In broad areas of Texas there were few whites to object to the entry of blacks. Lundy's dream was to establish a great territory to which blacks would be free to come if they wished and where they could get financial help to make a new start.

After three years of negotiations with the Mexican Government, Lundy was promised land as soon as he brought settlers. He returned happily to the

United States, only to fall seriously ill. When he recovered, he found that much had changed at home while he had been in Mexico. Other men, especially Garrison, were now leading a new and stronger abolition movement. They wanted no part of Lundy's plans for Texas. They saw these plans as one more scheme to rid the country of blacks.

In 1836 the Americans who had settled Texas, most of whom were proslavery Southerners, rebelled against the Mexican Government, hoping to make Texas an independent, slaveholding republic. There would be no land in Texas for Lundy, no dreamed-of free black domain.

While Americans cheered on the Texas rebels as brothers fighting for their independence, Lundy wrote a series of articles describing the Texans as slaveowners who conspired to overthrow the legitimate Mexican Government in order to make Texas a slave nation. He predicted that the next move would be to annex Texas to the United States, so that it would become an enormous addition to the American slave domain.

Lundy's articles came to the attention of John Quincy Adams, former president of the United States, and now a member of the House of Representatives. Adams quoted them in a series of powerful antislavery speeches in Congress. The two men met and Adams listened to Lundy with respect. Lundy, so often burdened by poverty and failure, was proud and happy. In a glow of optimism he founded a new magazine, *The National Enquirer,* to be published in Philadelphia, where he helped to organize a Pennsylvania Anti-Slavery Society. Speakers at its first meeting praised Lundy as the pioneer of abolitionism in the United States.

Lundy was by no means an old man now—not quite fifty, in fact—but illness and hardship had worn him out, and he had become so deaf he could take little active part in affairs. Once more his newspaper was a financial failure. His children, whom he had seen only infrequently for years, had moved to Illinois. It was time for him to give up and move there too, where he could be near them and live out the rest of his life in peace. He arranged to have a young abolitionist poet, John Greenleaf Whittier, take over as editor of *The National Enquirer.* All his clothes, personal property, books, and papers were moved to Pennsylvania Hall for safekeeping until his departure.

In the hall was a meeting of an association of women opposed to slavery. Men and women, black and white, mingled and spoke there. Outside, a mob of Philadelphians formed, outraged at the demonstration of racial and sexual equality and at the antislavery speeches. They broke in and burned the building and everything in it. Only one small box of Lundy's papers, including the diary he had kept in Mexico, was saved.

The weary, broken man made his way to Illinois. He bought a small farm which he worked himself. His twins lived with him and his other children lived nearby. He even found a friend, an unmarried

Quaker woman, to whom he wrote shy love poetry. He looked forward to marrying again and beginning a new life.

In the summer of 1839, after he had been in Illinois a year, he fell ill. He continued to work in his office, however, until he collapsed on August 21. The next day he died.

When William Lloyd Garrison heard of Lundy's death, he introduced a resolution to the Massachusetts Anti-Slavery Society stating that "to no man is the country so deeply indebted for the mighty impulse it has received on the subject of abolition, as the first cause of all protracted effort for the overthrow of slavery."

Slavery was more a part of American life than ever at the time of Lundy's death. But he had been a pioneer, a lone voice, the first of many vigorous men and women to lead the struggle for the abolition of slavery and the equality of black and white.

III

WILLIAM LLOYD GARRISON and the FOUNDING of the ABOLITION MOVEMENT in NEW ENGLAND

WILLIAM LLOYD GARRISON, the young man who had been so moved by Benjamin Lundy, burned with a determination to change the world. As a child, his personal world had not been a pleasant one. Garrison's father abandoned the family when the boy was only two years old, and he grew up desperately poor. His mother worked as a nurse in the homes of the rich merchants of Newburyport, Massachusetts. Young Lloyd had to come to their back doors, pail in hand, to beg for food. He was apprenticed to a shoemaker and to other tradespeople. For much of the time his mother worked in Baltimore while Garrison remained in Newburyport and Boston. Finally, he was apprenticed to a printer, and for the first time he found the kind of work that fulfilled him. He learned to set type and he became a swift, able printer. But he loved most the words that went into type. He wrote anonymous pieces and sent them to the newspapers. It was a great thrill when they were accepted for publication and he could set them in type himself with no one knowing he was the author.

The young printer wanted a cause to fight for; Lundy gave it to him at the gathering of ministers in the Boston boarding house, and the rest of Garrison's life was devoted to the fight for human freedom and equality. It took many forms; but his main goal was the abolition of slavery.

His first chance to play a serious role in the fight came in his work with Lundy in Baltimore. When he was released from the Baltimore jail after his experience with Lundy's newspaper, Garrison returned to Boston. He wanted a newspaper of his own, which might carry his words across the whole country and preserve them in the permanence of print.

Friends who had heard Garrison speak out against slavery raised a little money. A printer who had been his roommate agreed to be his partner. A religious newspaper let him use its type. The new year of 1831 began its first day with the proud first issue of "THE LIBERATOR, Wm. Lloyd Garrison, Editor." In the editorial for that issue the twenty-five-year-old Garrison said what he would do:

> I am aware, that many object to the severity of my language; but is there not cause for severity? I *will be* as harsh as truth, and as uncompromising

> as justice. On this subject I do not wish to think, or speak, or write, with moderation. No! no! Tell a man whose house is on fire, to give a moderate alarm; tell him to moderately rescue his wife from the hands of the ravisher; tell the mother to gradually extricate her babe from the fire into which it has fallen;—but urge me not to use moderation in a cause like the present. I am in earnest—I will not equivocate—I will not excuse—I will not retreat a single inch—AND I WILL BE HEARD.

In August 1831, a few months after *The Liberator* was founded, a slave named Nat Turner led a rebellion in which about sixty white men, women, and children were killed. Turner and his small band of followers were quickly seized, tried, and executed; but his uprising spread terror throughout the South. It had occurred in a quiet corner of southeastern Virginia, where slaves were treated less harshly than in other regions and where the work was relatively light. Turner himself had even been taught to read and write. If such hatred smouldered within the blacks of Virginia, what might the slaves feel on the rice, sugar, and cotton plantations farther south, where slavery was at its harshest and gangs were driven to hard labor in constant fear of the whip—and where slaves far outnumbered their masters? The South reacted with panic, and white Southerners regarded as an outright assassin anyone who might stir slaves to rise up.

Garrison opposed violence, even in self-defense, and he never urged slaves to use force to gain their freedom. But in Nat Turner's case, all his anger was directed at the slaveowners. Turner's men had done nothing worse, Garrison said, than did Americans who killed oppressive British soldiers at the time of the Revolution. To furious and frightened Southerners it sounded as though Garrison were comparing Nat Turner with George Washington. They remembered that *The Liberator* had praised David Walker's *Appeal*, which urged slaves to use force if they could gain their freedom in no other way.

Garrison sent free copies of *The Liberator* widely to officials in the South; many Southerners blamed him for the Turner uprising and believed he wanted to cause similar uprisings throughout the region. Several southern states accused him of crimes and offered rewards for his capture.

The following summer Garrison, at age twenty-seven the best-known abolitionist writer in the nation, met with a few of his friends and formed the New England Anti-Slavery Society. The new organization was more militant than earlier ones. It called slavery an intolerable sin and demanded its total and immediate abolition without compromises of any kind.

Garrison next attacked the colonization movement, which had drawn the support of many people opposed to slavery. He published his *Thoughts on African Colonization;* in it he condemned the supporters of colonization for protecting slavery by exiling the free blacks who might encourage slaves to seek their own freedom.

The following year he went to England, which

had become the center of the worldwide antislavery movement. English abolitionists were not poor men like Lundy and Garrison; they included members of the nobility and men of great wealth. A strong organization had fought for decades and succeeded in stopping the African slave trade. Now the abolitionists seemed to be persuading Parliament to abolish slavery in the British West Indies. What Garrison yearned for was to be recognized by the British abolitionists as a fellow leader and as the spokesman of American abolition.

The announced reason for Garrison's trip was to raise money to establish a school for free Negroes; but he did not collect even enough to pay his own expenses. He had spent his time instead arranging to meet British antislavery leaders and making public addresses attacking both slavery and some distinguished English advocates of colonization. He made enemies, but he made friends as well. Most important, he did come to be regarded in England as the leader of the American antislavery movement.

As soon as Garrison returned to the United States in September 1833 he turned to the formation of a national antislavery society. On December 4, 1833, in a howling snow storm, a few dozen abolitionists met in Philadelphia to form the American Anti-Slavery Society. The New York delegation, conservative in its approach, wanted to make sure the fiery Garrison did not take over the new organization. Garrison was not named to run it, but he was made responsible for corresponding with antislavery organizations in other countries and for drafting the society's basic principles. He produced an eloquent document which was modeled on the Declaration of Independence. It expressed the principles Garrison stood for: The society was to be for total emancipation immediately, everywhere, without any compensation to the slaveowners; blacks were equal in every way to whites and entitled to the same rights; the society would carry on an active program, including organizing local antislavery societies, training and sending out abolitionist lecturers, publishing tracts against slavery, and trying to convert ministers and newspaper editors to abolitionism. The declaration of principles was enthusiastically accepted by the members; Garrison, not yet thirty years old, had the organization he wanted and had nationwide publication for *The Liberator*. Now he could take a bit of time to marry Helen Benson, the daughter of a Connecticut abolitionist.

In 1835 one of Garrison's English friends, George Thompson, an abolitionist whose attacks on slavery and slaveowners were as violent as Garrison's, came to the United States. His lectures to Bostonians angered many who did not want to face the disturbing issue. Memories of the Revolution against England and the War of 1812 were still bitter. To many, Thompson seemed an arrogant Englishman attacking the United States and its institutions.

The Boston Female Anti-Slavery Society had invited Thompson and Garrison to speak on October 21, despite the possibility of a riot. When the day arrived, Thompson was not even in Boston, having been warned by friends to stay away because of threats to his life.

When Garrison arrived at the meeting room, he saw a group of men shouting and threatening the women there. Garrison managed to quiet them for a moment, the meeting started, and he slipped out and locked himself in the offices of the Anti-Slavery Society, which was in the same building. The mob started raging again; the meeting was adjourned; and the frustrated protestors decided to go after Garrison. They kicked in the door of his office just as he scrambled out the window and hid behind a pile of lumber. But they quickly found him and tied him up. There were threats to tar and feather him or hang him. Garrison fully expected to be killed.

Finally, he was brought to the office of Boston's mayor, who decided that jail was the only safe place for Garrison that night. On the wall of his cell he scratched a message saying that he had been kept there to protect him from "a 'respectable and influential' mob, who sought to destroy me for preaching the abominable and dangerous doctrine, that all men are created equal."

The incident made Garrison more famous. Many leading Americans, especially in New England, who had little or no sympathy with Garrison's views were appalled at the attacks on freedom of speech and assembly. It was becoming clear that slavery threatened the liberty of all people.

Garrison's sense of his own mission expanded. Not only was it wrong for whites to oppress blacks, every use of power to subject one person to another's will was wrong. The inequality of men and women was wrong. Military force was wrong. There should be no armies or navies, no guns or uniforms. Since all government was based ultimately on the use of power to enforce obedience, all government was wrong. Men and women, Garrison now believed, should give passive obedience to the laws, but should do nothing to cooperate with government. They should not hold office or serve in the militia, even when drafted, or serve on juries, or even vote. The only rightful authority on earth was that of Christ.

Naturally enough, these views, spread across the nation in *The Liberator*, got Garrison into trouble. He befriended two sisters from South Carolina, Sarah and Angelina Grimké, who had turned against the system of slavery in which they had grown up. Garrison encouraged them to speak to general audiences as well as to women's groups. The idea of women as public leaders and speakers offended many older and more conservative opponents of slavery.

Abolitionist clergymen issued a pamphlet criticizing Garrison, for they believed that he was weakening the abolitionist cause by tying it to other controversial issues, such as women's rights, and also by his reckless personal attacks on fellow opponents of slavery when they did not agree with him in every particular.

Garrison rejoiced in these attacks. Nothing did more to convince him that he was doing the right thing, and doing it effectively, than the outrage of his enemies. At the age of thirty-two, he had become the very symbol of total opposition to slavery. He happily accepted as a tribute the hatred of those who did not share his views.

Under his leadership Boston had become the center of the abolition movement. The New England Anti-Slavery Society he had founded remained the most vigorous and intense of the organized enemies of slavery. Men and women inspired by Garrison were to be the leaders and orators and philosophers of abolition throughout its history.

★IV★

The ABOLITIONISTS of NEW YORK and the WEST

THE Tappan brothers, Arthur and Lewis, two hardheaded businessmen, sought no enemies. Born in Northampton, Massachusetts, after the American Revolution, they came to New York and entered business as silk wholesalers. They were intensely religious men, who believed that people must govern their lives by Christ's teachings, and they practiced absolute honesty in their business dealings. In a day when the practice was still unusual, they had a single fixed price for everything they sold, and every customer paid the same. Their reputation for quality and integrity helped them to succeed in their business and grow wealthy.

The brothers believed that those whom God had blessed with financial success had a special obligation to use their money for human good. They contributed to many social and religious causes, but most of all to the fight against slavery. For of all man's sins, they thought slavery to be the worst.

It was Arthur Tappan who had arranged to have Garrison released from jail when he had been arrested in Baltimore and who helped him with funds to start *The Liberator*. The brothers also took the lead in forming a national organization to fight slavery. When the American Anti-Slavery Society was created in 1833, Arthur Tappan was elected its first president and Lewis Tappan became one of its secretaries. For years the Tappans were major financial supporters of the organization. They also spent long hours at the society's office, addressing and mailing pamphlets, doing bookkeeping, carrying on correspondence. And they brought many of their wealthy friends with them into the antislavery movement.

Both Tappans believed fervently that blacks and whites equally were children of God and that prejudice against blacks in the North was a sin just as was slavery in the South. Lewis Tappan declared: "We must eat, walk, travel, and worship with people of color and show to slaveholders and their abettors at the North, that we will recognize them as brothers." He often entertained blacks in his home, and insisted on integrated seating in churches and at abolitionist meetings.

The Tappans refused to eat sugar made from cane grown by slaves. They would not buy or sell cotton in their business and tried to avoid using slave-produced goods in their daily lives. They helped fugitive slaves to escape, defended them against their former owners, and paid the legal bills of free Negroes who slaveowners claimed were fugitives.

They suffered physical abuse for their beliefs. When the New York Anti-Slavery Society was created in 1833, a mob attempted to break up its first meeting. Arthur Tappan, who had been elected president of the organization, barely escaped their attack and the church building in which they met was badly damaged. Arthur Tappan had been assaulted as early as 1831. In July 1834 Lewis Tappan was stoned in the street. His home was broken into and his furniture hauled out. The next day the Tappans' warehouse and store were almost destroyed. But the brothers drew strength and courage from their religion, and particularly from their association with Charles Grandison Finney, a minister from upstate New York.

New York State's Mohawk Valley, stretching westward from Albany toward Niagara Falls, was one of the most religious areas in the country. Ministers were always traveling over the region, preaching emotional sermons full of threats of eternal hellfire. In fact, part of the area was known as the "Burned-Over District" because it has so often been swept by religious revivals, accompanied by fiery sermons.

Finney was one of the fieriest of these preachers. He had been a lawyer who was later ordained a Presbyterian minister. With no church of his own, he traveled over upstate New York, holding revival meetings that might last for days or weeks. For hours he would bring the congregation before him face-to-face with horrible visions of hell, so vivid that many would fall to the floor, crying out to be saved. Finney demanded that they accept Christ and also devote themselves to helping their fellow men. His converts made up the backbone of many reform movements, especially opposition to drunkenness and slavery.

As a result of these intense religious convictions antislavery feelings took early root throughout the Mohawk Valley. Rochester and Utica became centers of abolitionist activity. A wealthy upstate farmer, Gerrit Smith, provided money for many antislavery efforts and late in his life became the Radical Abolitionist candidate for president of the United States.

Much of the money and leadership for the organization of the national antislavery movement came from New York. But the abolitionists there were always more conservative than Garrison and the New Englanders he led. The New Yorkers were just as opposed to slavery, but they were loyal members of the established churches; they tried to work for change within the established political system and they opposed such movements as pacifism and women's rights, which were dear to Garrison. They were concerned less about being free personally from any stain of acceptance of slavery than with finding practical steps to end it. As time went on, they and Garrison would move further and further apart.

While Garrison led the New England abolitionists

and electrified the country with *The Liberator,* and the Tappans and their friends began organizing in New York, another movement was starting in the West. It was led by Theodore Dwight Weld, a young New Englander who could concentrate so intently on a thought that he forgot everything else.

Weld was born in Connecticut in 1802, three years before Garrison, to a family of Congregational ministers. He was tall and strong, with a great mass of tousled hair he rarely combed. As a student at the Phillips Academy, in Andover, Massachusetts, Weld tried to do two years' work in one, nearly ruined his eyesight, and was forced to drop out when he was seventeen. He had been impressed by a system for improving the memory, of which he had learned at Andover. After thorough study, he began to travel about giving lectures on it. He did well, earning a comfortable living and coming to know New England and its people. He also discovered he was a natural platform speaker. With practice, Weld learned to hold and sway almost any audience. He extended his lecture tours farther and farther—westward to Ohio, south through Maryland, the District of Columbia, Virginia, and North Carolina. Here he first saw slavery on a large scale. It offended him but did not yet arouse his moral outrage.

Weld lectured for three years, then entered Hamilton College in upstate New York. Here he heard Charles Grandison Finney speak, was electrified by him, and became Finney's disciple and assistant. Though Finney opposed slavery, it was not the center of his interest. What he gave Weld was an intense commitment to spend all his strength fighting sin.

Weld transferred to Oneida Institute, a Bible college in the area. He continued to show his great ability as a speaker in the surrounding towns and villages, where he raised money for the institute, demanded strict observance of the Sabbath, and assaulted drunkenness.

The young speaker was becoming well known. He was called to New York by Lewis Tappan, who knew of him through Finney. Tappan wanted to interest Weld in fighting slavery. Though Weld was not yet ready to become a minister, as the Tappans wished, or to devote all his effort to fighting slavery, he became involved in another of Tappans' interests, manual labor instruction in academies and colleges.

When Lewis Tappan could not persuade Weld to become an abolitionist preacher, he made him a general agent of the Society for Promoting Manual Labor in Literary Institutions. For the next year Weld traveled widely, studying manual education experiments wherever they could be found and speaking almost daily in support of the movement and of other causes, such as the fight against drunkenness. He journeyed all through the Middle West and down into the South, through Kentucky, Tennessee, and Alabama, saw slavery again, and ended his travels at the Western Reserve College, near Cleveland, Ohio. This was a newly founded institution with a strong New England tradition. Charles Storrs, the president, and key members of the faculty, such as

Beriah Green and Elizur Wright, were abolitionists and followers of Garrison. In his stay at Western Reserve Weld was converted at last to a belief in the need for immediate abolition.

He returned to New York and resigned his position as general agent for the Society for Promoting Manual Labor in Literary Institutions. Determined now to complete his education, enter the ministry, and devote his life to fighting slavery, Weld entered the newly founded Lane Institute in Cincinnati, Ohio. Lane was a manual education school set up to train ministers for the growing West. Most of its students were in their mid-twenties or older; they were serious, idealistic, and dedicated men.

Cincinnati was located just across the Ohio River from Kentucky, a slave state. Radical issues swirled through it. Escaping slaves crossed into Cincinnati on their way to Canada. There was also a large free Negro population in the city, but Cincinnati's blacks lived in poverty and fear because white leaders and businessmen had close contacts with Kentucky planters and were generally proslavery and anti-black.

In the spring of 1834, moved largely by Weld, Lane's students ran a series of debates on abolition and colonization. For eighteen consecutive nights the students united in denouncing the colonization movement and demanding immediate abolition. They formed a local antislavery society, and they decided to help the free blacks around them in Cincinnati. They volunteered as teachers and nurses, collected money for food and clothing, and worked in the black community. Many of them lived as paying boarders in black homes.

The president and faculty of Lane were not prepared for the students' radical stand. When school started in the fall of 1834, the students were told to abandon their discussions of slavery and to stop their work with blacks, which offended leading citizens of Cincinnati and supporters of the school. The students refused. The active members of the antislavery society, Weld among them, left or were expelled.

The Tappans shifted their financial support to an even newer school at Oberlin, Ohio. Oberlin, which accepted black students from its beginning, was founded on thoroughly abolitionist principles. Most of the students who left Lane enrolled here.

Weld, however, was ready to devote his full time to abolition, without further schooling. He became an agent of the American Anti-Slavery Society. He traveled the state of Ohio tirelessly, making speeches and organizing local antislavery societies wherever he went. In April 1835 he took the lead in forming a statewide Ohio Anti-Slavery Society. Abolition, which was almost unknown in Ohio a year or two before, was now a strong and growing movement throughout the state.

Weld moved on to western Pennsylvania and upstate New York to carry the fight there. He lectured day and night, often facing mobs which threatened him and pelted him with rotten eggs. Again he made converts wherever he spoke and left behind him active antislavery groups. Within two years hundreds of groups had been established across the northern states.

The effort wore him out and reduced his powerful voice to a croaking whisper. Weld had to give up speaking. He spent the following months working in the office of the American Anti-Slavery Society handling correspondence and editing pamphlets. But his disciples were everywhere, carrying the abolitionist message into every corner of the country. They were Weld's army, matching Garrison's words in *The Liberator,* mobilizing abolition in the United States.

Back in 1832, when Weld had visited Alabama, one of the men he met was a tall, handsome, wealthy, slaveowning planter and lawyer named James G. Birney. Originally from Kentucky, Birney had decided to try his fortune in the booming new state of Alabama. Here he served in the first legislature, was one of the founders of the state university, and had been the mayor of Huntsville, the principal town of northern Alabama.

But Birney was a troubled man. Though he had grown up in a society in which no one questioned slavery, his conscience bothered him, and he had made his concern known. At the time he met Weld he had been invited to work for the American Colonization Society. Weld himself still approved the idea of colonization and urged Birney to accept. He did, leaving his law practice and for a year traveling throughout the region, speaking, conferring with local leaders, writing articles for the press. He had little success. Even Birney's very mild criticism of slavery was no longer tolerated in the South.

Discouraged, Birney moved back to Kentucky, still hoping that at least those southern states that bordered on freedom—Maryland, Kentucky, and Virginia—could be persuaded to do away with the institution. He freed all his own slaves and came out as vigorously as had Garrison against the colonization movement, for which he had so recently worked. "Colonization," he said, "has done more to rock the conscience of the slaveholder into slumber, and to make his slumber soft and peaceful, than all other causes united."

Birney got in close touch with Weld. He now took a job as agent for the American Anti-Slavery Society and formed the Kentucky Anti-Slavery Society, a tiny organization committed to immediate abolition. He then went to Ohio, where he helped Weld organize the Ohio Anti-Slavery Society, and on to Boston. He was hailed as a hero everywhere in the North. No other Southerner of his standing and ability had ever joined the antislavery movement.

Birney returned to Kentucky in the summer of 1835, determined to publish an antislavery newspaper at his home in Danville. But threats of violence forced the owner of the printing press to refuse to work for Birney. Unhappily, he moved to Cincinnati, where in January 1836 he began the publication of the newspaper he had planned, *The Philanthropist.* He quickly found that even Cincinnati was not ready for an abolitionist newspaper.

Newspaper editorials attacked him and a public meeting was called to denounce his proposal. Birney appealed to Cincinnatians to respect the freedom of the press. He managed to publish *The Philanthropist* for a little while, but in the hot summer days that followed a gang broke into the printing office and damaged the press. Then, one night, a group of men took the press apart, dumped it in the Ohio River, destroyed the office, and wrecked much of the black section of the city.

A new press was acquired and publication of *The Philanthropist* was resumed, but Birney was sickened by the atmosphere in Cincinnati. He was offered the post of corresponding secretary of the American Anti-Slavery Society. This would put him at the center of the campaign to organize the antislavery movement throughout the country. He accepted it gladly, and in 1837 moved with his family to New York.

★V★

SLAVERY FIGHTS BACK

THROUGH the years, from Woolman to Garrison, abolitionists had seen slavery primarily as a moral and religious problem. Slavery was a sin, a terrible sin. The early abolitionists were religious people, Quakers or evangelical Protestants. They believed a Christian should take no part in that sin, should keep free from any stain of slavery.

Their next responsibility, they thought, was to bring the message of the sinfulness of slavery to slaveowners, so that they would free their slaves. Early abolitionists, such as Woolman, tried to come to the slaveowners in love and understanding. Later ones, such as Garrison, wrote and spoke in anger. The style of all of them, though, was like that of revivalist ministers, who tried to shock sinners into conversion and salvation by showing them the horror of their sins. It was the sinners, the slaveholders, these abolitionists wanted to reach. So most of them began their work in the South.

Some Southerners had been criticizing slavery openly for a long time. Thomas Jefferson denounced it as an evil and a sin. George Washington expressed his opposition to slavery and freed his own slaves. Societies to encourage the freeing of slaves, if not the end of slavery, existed all through the South in the early 1800s. The American Colonization Society was strongest in the South. Benjamin Lundy published his antislavery newspaper in Tennessee and Maryland. As late as 1829 a convention to draw up a new constitution for Virginia debated provisions for the gradual elimination of slavery in the state.

Around 1830 things changed. Any criticism became intolerable. The cotton boom and the settlement of Alabama and Mississippi made slavery and the plantation system very profitable. There were now more than two million slaves in the United States. Nat Turner's small rebellion spread the fear of blacks—especially *uncontrolled* ones—across the South. Even those Southerners who had thought of slavery as a necessary evil, to be limited wherever possible and ultimately to be done away with, now began calling it a good practice that should be strengthened, extended, and made permanent.

Anything that might lead blacks to think they had a right to be free now was regarded with horror by southern leaders. It was not that abolitionist publications tried to stir blacks to revolt. On the contrary, they almost always urged slaves to bear their lot quietly and preached Christian forgiveness toward the masters. The slaveowners, however, moved to stop any antislavery publications, however mild, from coming into the South. The American Anti-Slavery Society, as soon as it was formed in 1833, started publishing leaflets, newspapers, and pamphlets and distributing them throughout the country. They wanted especially to spread them through the South, not to rouse up slaves, but to persuade their masters that slavery was an evil thing that should be ended voluntarily.

When shipment of these publications arrived in Charleston, South Carolina, in 1835, the local citizens marched into the post office, seized the bundles, and burned them. They set up a committee to go over all incoming publications and tell the postmaster which could be delivered and which he must destroy. The postmaster, instead of arresting the pamphlet-burners for robbing the United States mails, asked the postmaster general in Washington what to do. Postmaster General Amos Kendall said he could not legally tell the Charleston postmaster *not* to deliver such publications, but neither would he order him *to* deliver them: the obligation of postmasters to their local communities was more important than their obligation to the law.

Southern representatives tried to get Congress to enact a law keeping antislavery publications from the mails. Congress refused. Nevertheless, every southern state forbade the delivery of such publications, and the federal government made no effort to deliver them against local objections.

To make sure that no abolitionist publications were smuggled in, the southern states passed laws punishing any person who distributed them. The ban on printed criticism of slavery was enforced by jail sentences and mob violence.

Amos Dresser, a student at Lane Seminary, journeyed through the South selling Bibles in the summer of 1835. In Nashville, Tennessee, a mob broke into his room and found some old copies of an antislavery newspaper in which Dresser wrapped his Bibles. He was whipped in the public square and driven from the city.

By the late 1830s there was no way to reach the slaveowners. Abolitionists and their publications simply could not get into the South. And the slave-owners and traders, making great profit from their system, had no wish to hear of abolition.

Moreover, almost everyone, whether for or against slavery, agreed that the Constitution recognized and protected slavery in the states. Under the Constitution the Congress could not, and the slave-state legislatures clearly would not, take any action to end slavery.

There was one way left to move against slavery. Congress might not be able to do anything about slavery within the states; but Congress, if it chose, could abolish slavery in the District of Columbia and the territories, could forbid slaves to be sold from one state to another, and could let no state into the Union in the future if its constitution permitted slavery.

If they could not reach the slaveowners, the abolitionists decided they would try to reach Congress. They sent petitions to every session of Congress urging laws to limit or end slavery. But now the South was determined to suppress all discussion of slavery even in Congress. In 1836 southern members pushed a "gag rule" through the House of Representatives, preventing all petitions having to do with slavery from being read or discussed. It turned out to be a mistake. Northerners who had not cared about blacks began to worry about the loss of their own liberty. They grew angry at what some saw as a "southern conspiracy" to take over the government, for the supporters of slavery seemed willing to suppress all freedom—of speech, of the press, of petition—in order to protect their power to buy, sell, and own other human beings.

And the gag rule did not stop the petitions; it brought an increase in them. Although the petitions could not be discussed, the existence of the rule itself gave much opportunity for debate. So did the question of whether any given petition came under the rule. John Greenleaf Whittier, the poet, ran a campaign for the American Anti-Slavery Society to gather as many petitions as possible. From December 1838 to March 1839, nearly fifteen hundred petitions were sent to Congress. Some one hundred fifty thousand people had signed them.

Inside Congress the opposition to the gag rule was led by former President John Quincy Adams, now a representative from Massachusetts. Despite threats to expel him from the House of Representatives, Adams battled against the gag rule and encouraged thousands of Americans to join him. Not until 1844, after eight years, did he win his fight.

There were determined efforts to shut off attacks on slavery in the North as well. We know that Lewis Tappan was stoned in the streets of New York, his house ransacked, and the Tappans' store attacked; that a mob nearly hung Garrison in the streets of Boston; and that the Cincinnati print shop producing Birney's newspaper was wrecked by riots. According to newspaper accounts, there were at least one hundred sixty-five attacks on antislavery speakers or publications in the North between 1833 and 1838.

When the young antislavery speakers trained by Weld spread out across the North in the mid-1830s they were met almost everywhere by mobs armed with stones and rotten eggs, and sometimes with whips and guns. Many an antislavery speaker had to clean the stinking eggs from his one good suit and hope that by hanging his clothes to dry in the sun he could remove the lingering odor. The American Anti-Slavery Society trained its agents not to fight back or resist, but to stand with arms folded when threatened. Few mobs could bring themselves to attack a man who stood before them defenseless but unafraid. Though none of the agents was killed or even seriously injured, many were bruised and beaten or driven out of town, their clothes torn, their papers scattered and destroyed. Every agent knew he risked his life with every speech. They were prepared to die to carry their call for freedom through the country.

The violence got worse. In St. Louis in 1836 a mob burned a black prisoner to death. Elijah P. Lovejoy, editor of *The Observer,* called it "Awful Murder . . . Savage Barbarity" in his newspaper, and criticized the judge who went easy on the killers. Lovejoy's life was threatened. He moved to Alton, Illinois, where many New Englanders who were opposed to slavery had settled. A band of men from St. Louis followed him to Alton and destroyed his press and type as they stood on the dock. Lovejoy raised the money for a new press.

The Illinois state legislature had just recognized the constitutional right of the southern states to maintain slavery and had condemned antislavery agitation. But the abolition movement was also growing in Illinois. Lovejoy's paper quickly became its center. Proslavery men decided to silence *The Observer.* They broke into Lovejoy's office and once more destroyed the press. Lovejoy ordered a third press. This never reached him; it was thrown into the river as it was being unloaded from the boat.

A forth press was ordered. This time Lovejoy's friends were determined that he would get it and continue publishing *The Observer.* A statewide convention to set up an Illinois Anti-Slavery Society was planned for Alton; the newspaper was essential to its success. An armed band of Lovejoy's supporters met the boat and brought the press to a stone warehouse with few windows, where it would be kept until it could be put up in Lovejoy's office.

A crowd of angry proslavery men gathered around the warehouse. Hours passed. Suddenly, someone outside fired a shot. A rifle cracked in answer from the warehouse. Soon there was steady gunfire from both sides. A scream, and one of the proslavery crowd fell dead. His comrades, now in a fury, placed a ladder against the warehouse. A man started climbing toward the roof, carrying a burning brand. A few abolitionists ran out of the building, firing their guns at him. The climber slid down the ladder. Some of the mob crawled behind a lumber pile, where they were protected, and opened fire on the defenders. The climber started back up. This time he reached the roof and set it aflame.

Lovejoy and one of his friends darted from the building and raised their pistols toward the man on the ladder. Before they could fire, Lovejoy was hit by five bullets. He staggered to the door and crawled to the warehouse office. Here he fell dead.

The mob swarmed into the building and pushed the press from a third-floor window. It crashed to the street, where men seized it, dragged it to the wharf, smashed it to pieces with hammers and threw the parts into the river.

No one had the courage to take Lovejoy's place and publish an antislavery paper in Alton. But the bloody night greatly strengthened the abolition movement. Throughout the country angry meetings were held to protest Lovejoy's murder. Thousands of men and women who had not been abolitionists and would have been willing to leave slavery undisturbed in the South were shocked by the deadly attack on freedom of the press. They became convinced that those who supported slavery were denying freedom to whites as well as to blacks. Lovejoy was mourned as a martyr of the antislavery movement. The American Anti-Slavery Society began to use a letterhead that read: "LOVEJOY the first MARTYR to American LIBERTY. MURDERED for asserting the FREEDOM OF THE PRESS, Alton Nov. 7, 1837."

Lovejoy's death reduced the antagonism toward abolition in the North, and the use of violence against northern abolitionists dropped sharply. In a few years, abolitionists throughout the northern states could write and speak as they chose, could freely hold meetings, and publish their newspapers.

A few abolitionists had even been elected to Congress by 1844, when the gag rule was repealed. In the House of Representatives they included William Slade of Vermont and Joshua Giddings of Ohio; in the Senate, Thomas Morris, also of Ohio. There were also some members of Congress who were friendly to the antislavery cause and would vote with the abolitionists on many issues. Among them was, of course, John Quincy Adams. They could never carry a vote in the House or in the Senate, but their words could have an impact on the nation.

The abolitionists needed research help though, because the supporters of slavery had denied their charges about the cruelty of slaveowners and overseers and the suffering of slaves. Slaveholders said that slaves were almost always well cared for—even treated affectionately. The American Anti-Slavery Society provided assistance. It sent Theodore Weld to Washington. Weld, forceful and eloquent as ever, even though his voice had been ruined from the strain of daily antislavery speeches, did an enormous amount of research. He produced an impressive book, *American Slavery As It Is,* that assembled the facts from eyewitness testimony, official documents, and accounts taken from southern newspapers themselves. The book became a bible for the abolitionists in Congress and for editors and speakers throughout the country. In addition, Weld worked day and night in Washington doing legal research, writing memoranda, drafting speeches. He powered the congressional attack on slavery without ever serving as a member of Congress.

When Garrison began publishing *The Liberator* in 1831, there had been only a handful of abolitionists in the country. With few exceptions, leaders in the movement were whites, most of them deeply religious Quakers or New England Congregationalists. Many seemed to be fanatics, half-crazy with their impossible belief in freedom for blacks. Many were ministers. With a few exceptions such as the Tappans, they were poor and had no place near the center of power in society, in business, in government, or even in their churches.

After the 1830s the abolitionist cause became respectable in the North. Many prominent people began to give it their support. The way had opened for two major groups to join its ranks: blacks and women.

VI

BLACK ABOLITIONISTS

BLACKS, who suffered the most from slavery, had always been its bitterest foes. But until the 1830s there was relatively little they could do about it. Slaves had no freedom to travel or to meet. They could attack the system only by quietly sabotaging it in their daily work, by trying to escape to freedom, or by a rare desperate uprising. Free Negroes were not much better off; few of them had the education or the money to make major contributions to the abolition movement.

As the movement gained strength though, it helped more and more blacks to become members and effective leaders of abolitionist groups.

The most famous black abolitionist was Frederick Douglass. Born a slave in Maryland in 1817, Douglass learned to read as a child. Later, he was taken to Baltimore and hired out as a shipyard worker. He married a free black woman who saved part of her wages to help him escape; then he borrowed papers from a black seaman identifying him as a free black, boarded a train, and, after fearing that a close check of his papers would reveal he was a fugitive slave, arrived in New York.

Douglass was twenty years old, penniless, and alone in a strange city. It was 1838, and New York was in an economic depression. He was a skilled workman, but jobs were few and white men kept them for themselves. Douglass dared not go to the police or charities to ask for food and shelter; as a runaway slave, he could be arrested and taken back in chains to Maryland. He walked the streets until he nearly fell from hunger and exhaustion. Finally, in desperation, he stopped a black sailor and asked for help. The sailor sent him to David Ruggles.

Ruggles, an educated black man with at least a little money, had just started a magazine, *The Mirror of Liberty,* which may have been the first in the United States to be published by a black. More important for Douglass, Ruggles was a leader of the New York Vigilance Committee, an organization that helped runaway slaves and protected blacks from being seized under the fugitive slave laws.

Ruggles took Douglass into his own home, fed, clothed, and concealed him. He got word to Douglass's wife in Baltimore and arranged for her to join him in New York. Then he got them aboard a ship for New Bedford, Massachusetts, and arranged for a black couple there to help them find work and a place to live.

New Bedford's shipyards were closed to blacks; so Douglass got jobs as a longshoreman, a chimney sweep, a waiter, a coachman. Young as he was, he began to take a leading part in the small but educated and prosperous black community of New Bedford. He joined a black church. He subscribed to Garrison's *The Liberator,* and he began to go to abolitionist meetings. He soon became the leader of the little black abolitionist group in New Bedford.

In 1841, when he was twenty-four, he attended a meeting in New Bedford of the Bristol County Anti-Slavery Society. Here he met William Lloyd Garrison, already a hero to Douglass. Garrison was impressed with the intelligent, earnest, handsome young black man. Perhaps it was Garrison who arranged to have Douglass called on to speak the next day at the Massachusetts Anti-Slavery Society's convention on Nantucket Island. Caught by surprise, Douglass spoke awkwardly about his own life as a slave. His simple words were very moving, and they formed the subject of Garrison's fiery speech that followed. On the spot Douglass was asked to become a paid lecturer and agent for the Massachusetts Anti-Slavery Society.

At first he was brought to abolitionist meetings to show how blacks could improve themselves if given a chance. Few New England abolitionists had ever met a black, no less one who had been a slave, and it was exciting to hear a first-hand account of slavery. Even those abolitionists most sympathetic to blacks sometimes accepted the general view that they were an unintelligent and childlike people who must be looked after and protected by their white friends. Douglass was a living denial of this myth. He was striking in appearance—a tall, strong body, a great mass of hair, flashing eyes, and a rich, powerful voice. His speech grew eloquent and soon Douglass became one of the outstanding orators and leaders of the abolition movement.

For the next years Douglass lectured almost daily for the Massachusetts, American, Rhode Island, and New England Anti-Slavery Societies. He also wrote his autobiography, *Narrative of the Life of Frederick Douglass,* a short, moving book. Published in 1845, it made Douglass, still in his twenties, nationally famous.

With his earnings from the book, Douglass decided to visit antislavery leaders in England. Several years before, in 1833, the British Parliament had ended slavery throughout the British Empire, including the West Indies.

In September 1845, Douglass sailed for England without his family. He stayed there for nearly two years. Black American abolitionists were popular with the English, and Douglass came to know almost every significant British abolitionist. He even sold enough copies of his book to meet most of his expenses. Toward the end of his stay, some of his British friends raised the money to buy his freedom, so that he never again need fear capture. Douglass became so popular and famous in England that he was reluctant to return home. But finally he left, and when he returned to Massachusetts he received a warm welcome, with meetings and receptions held in his honor.

While in England, Douglass had decided to edit and publish an abolitionist newspaper. There were now several nationally known antislavery journals besides Garrison's *Liberator*. And although there were a few, small abolitionist newspapers edited and published by blacks, there was no really first-rate, national black paper. Young and inexperienced though he was, Douglass was confident he could produce one. It would give him a chance to make his views known throughout the country without the exhaustion, danger, and constant travel of the lecture tour. Douglass also believed that the example of a well-written, well-edited newspaper published by a former slave would be a great thing in itself; it would help to prove to the world that slaves, once freed and given an opportunity, could equal the intellect and accomplishments of anyone.

Douglass was surprised and discouraged when friends like Garrison tried to discourage him. Experienced men, who knew how desperately hard it was to put out an abolitionist newspaper and keep it going financially, they thought it unlikely that a young former slave, lacking formal education, newspaper experience, or money, could produce a successful newspaper. Douglass was also aware, however, that most of the subscribers to *The Liberator* were black, and might leave Garrison's newspaper for the new, black-sponsored one. To Douglass it sometimes seemed as if his white friends were telling him that it was fine to exhibit a former slave who could make speeches, but that anything difficult, like editing a newspaper, should be left to them.

At first Douglass took their advice and joined Garrison in another lecture tour of the West. In Cleveland Garrison collapsed from exhaustion and Douglass went ahead to finish the tour alone. Perhaps his success when he was on his own made him bolder. In any event, his views had come to differ from Garrison's. Douglass demanded forthright action against slavery, including political organization and even force when necessary in self-defense. He was unwilling to accept Garrison's total pacifism and rejection of political effort. He decided to break with Garrison and go ahead with his dream.

He selected Rochester, New York, a center of abolition, as the location of his newspaper. It was a rapidly growing young city, profiting from the traffic on the Erie Canal. No competing abolitionist newspaper was published there. In Massachusetts Douglass had sometimes felt almost smothered by Garrison and *The Liberator* and by the American Anti-Slavery Society. In Rochester he would be his own man. At the end of 1847 he moved his family to their new home and began the publication of his paper. He called it *The North Star*. The North Star was the beacon escaping slaves followed as they made their way to freedom through the darkness; it was a bright star that remained in the same unchanging position night after night.

Although Douglass was the most famous of the black abolitionist leaders, there were dozens of others. Some, such as Robert Purvis and James Forten, had made money and used it to aid the cause. Forten was a sailmaker who built a prosperous business in Philadelphia. He gave money to help Garrison's *Liberator* and other antislavery newspapers. As early as 1817, when the colonization movement was still supported by most opponents of slavery, Forten organized a meeting to attack the whole idea as an effort to send blacks into exile. In 1837 he was one of the founders of the Pennsylvania Anti-Slavery Society. He brought his children and grandchildren up to be educated, able antislavery leaders. Three of his daughters were founders of the Female Anti-Slavery Society of Philadelphia.

One of those daughters married Robert Purvis, who was himself well off, having inherited money from his wealthy white father. He was one of the three blacks at the 1833 meeting to organize the American Anti-Slavery Society and served for a number of years as head of the Pennsylvania Anti-Slavery Society. Purvis was especially active in helping runaway slaves: He was the chairman of the Philadelphia Vigilance Committee, formed to protect runaways, and his country home near Philadelphia was an important stop on the Underground Railroad. He fought not only against slavery, but for full equality for blacks, often refusing to attend segregated meetings.

One of the battles he lost was against a provision in the new Pennsylvania state constitution, adopted in 1838, which barred blacks from voting. In 1834 Purvis visited England and made an excellent impression with his social ease, handsome appearance, and keen intelligence.

Charles Lenox Remond was more militant than Forten or Purvis. As were many abolitionists, black and white, Remond was a minister. He was hired by the American Anti-Slavery Society in the 1830s to lecture all across the North. Black abolitionists were subject to even more threats and mob violence than were white speakers. But the barrage of bricks and rotten eggs Remond so often faced did not silence or frighten him; they made him more bitter and determined in his opposition to slavery.

Most white abolitionists were pacifists, who did not believe force should ever be used, even against evil. Most black abolitionists, including Remond, did not agree. As early as 1840 he was expressing the hope that America and Great Britain might go to war over Canada, as the turmoil might give slaves a chance to seize their freedom. He welcomed slave uprisings and was ready to use violence to protect or free fugitive slaves. He thought the American Constitution was a wicked document because it recognized slavery, and he was quite ready to see the Union dissolved if that would hasten the end of slavery. By the 1850s Remond was agitating for the enlistment and arming of black militia companies.

Henry Highland Garnet was even more militant than Remond. Garnet was born a slave in Maryland. When he was nine his family escaped and settled in New York, where he got a good education in an elementary school for blacks. When he was fourteen the family split up to avoid being found and sent back to Maryland. Garnet was apprenticed as a seaman, but before he completed his service he hurt his leg in an accident. For years the leg remained infected and painful. Stubbornly, Garnet went back to school, completed his education, and became a minister in New York. When he was twenty-five years old, in 1840, the leg had to be amputated. A tall and powerful man with a glistening ebony skin, Garnet was an imposing figure even on crutches.

Garnet threw himself into the abolitionist movement early. He was not willing simply to denounce slavery as a sin; he wanted to take concrete steps to end it. And he wanted action in the North to do away with the prejudice and discrimination faced by blacks even in the free states. Unlike Garrison, he cared less about ideals than about getting things done. Garrison and his followers denounced the churches, the government, and the Constitution. Garnet wanted to use government and the churches to help free Negros and to limit slavery wherever possible. Garrison thought abolitionists should not even vote because voting gave recognition to a corrupt government; Garnet fought hard to win the vote for free Negroes so that they could better their lot.

Garnet became discouraged in the early 1840s by the failure of abolition to achieve any of its goals. Slavery seemed more firmly established in the South than ever. Texas had become independent of Mexico and was a slave nation; its annexation to the

United States as a huge, powerful slave state seemed certain to come soon. In the northern states things were getting worse, not better. Laws were being passed to limit the freedom of blacks to live and work where they chose. Schools were segregated. New York in 1841 imposed stiff property requirements on blacks before they could vote, but made no such requirement for whites. Pennsylvania took away all the rights of blacks to vote.

In 1843, asked to address a convention of blacks meeting at Buffalo, New York, Garnet called his speech "An Address to Slaves," although few slaves would ever have a chance to read it or hear about it. It was not only the right but the duty of slaves to rise up and fight for their own freedom, he exclaimed: "Brethren, arise, arise! Strike for your lives and liberties. Now is the day and the hour. Let every slave throughout the land do this, and the days of slavery are numbered. You cannot be more oppressed than you have been—You cannot suffer greater cruelties than you have already. *Rather die freemen than live to be slaves.*"

His language was not very different from that used by white leaders at the time of the American Revolution, when Patrick Henry cried, "Give me liberty or give me death!" But it lost Garnet most of his support. For years southern whites had denounced abolitionists as firebrands who wanted slaves to murder their masters, and Garnet's words gave them evidence. Moderate and conservative antislavery leaders were frightened. Garrison and most of the radical abolitionists were pacifists who believed that one should never use violence; they too were shocked at Garnet's bold words.

Garnet had spoken out of desperation; but he was too practical and realistic ever to try to organize a hopeless and suicidal uprising. Though he never again urged slaves to rise, he continued to think they had a *right* to take arms and that the only reason they should not was if they did not have enough power to succeed. Meanwhile, he continued to be an inspiring minister, carried on his fight to improve the lives of northern blacks, and journeyed to England to lecture and attend antislavery meetings.

As the nation entered the 1850s, Garnet became more pessimistic about the future of blacks in the United States. Texas had now been annexed. War with Mexico had added another vast western territory, much of which would be open to slavery. An agreement in the Congress, called the Compromise of 1850, allowed the settlers in each new territory to decide whether they wanted slavery. As part of the Compromise, a new, harsh Fugitive Slave Law threatened the freedom not only of escaped former slaves but also of northern blacks born free but without records to prove it.

Garnet had bitterly opposed the American Colonization Society; it aimed, he believed, to banish free blacks from the United States. But now he came to feel that though blacks had every right to stay in the United States and live in freedom and equality, they might well prefer to move elsewhere rather than face the realities of American life. Perhaps black men and women might after all find in

Africa the equality, dignity, and opportunity denied them in America. All during the 1850s Garnet explored the possibility of settling American blacks in Liberia or other areas of Africa. But he did not reach that continent himself until 1881, when he became the American minister to Liberia. There he died and was buried.

Black women had always worked alongside black men in sharing the common burdens of slavery, and they shared as well the common dangers of the fight for freedom. In the north, black women—often, like the daughter of James Forten, well educated and with some means—took an active part in many female anti-slavery societies. But two of the most famous freedom fighters among black women were poor and illiterate former slaves, who became leaders through their own enormous courage and force of character.

One was a New Yorker, freed by that state's law emancipating all slaves on July 4, 1827. She called herself Sojourner Truth, and indeed she was a sojourner, going from place to place to speak out the truth. She became one of the most famous of abolitionist orators. Though she could not read or write, her sayings were copied down and published. She fought for the rights of women as well as blacks and was an early leader in the general women's rights movement.

An even greater role was played by one of the bravest of all antislavery leaders—Harriet Tubman. She was brought up as a slave in Maryland. Even as a child she fought so hard against being a slave that she was often beaten and was forced to do the heaviest work in the fields. In 1849, when she learned she was about to be sold to a slavedealer who would take her to the deep South, she escaped. Hiding by day and slipping along back roads by night, she made her way to Pennsylvania and freedom.

After winning her own freedom, she dedicated her life to leading others to liberty. The year after her escape she made her way back to Maryland to rescue her sister. In the following years she made trip after trip into the South and led about three hundred slaves to freedom. When the Civil War came she was asked to work along with the Union Army that had captured islands along the coast of South Carolina and Georgia. She helped hundreds of slaves to escape from plantations on the mainland and helped to plan and inspire inland raids by the Union forces. She lived to be a very old woman working hard to add to a tiny pension, but remaining a symbol of brave devotion to human rights until her death in 1913.

Black abolitionists worked against enormous prejudices. Even those whites who opposed slavery often did not accept blacks as equals. Outside of New England white abolitionists resisted any black's holding office or exercising leadership in an antislavery organization. No black ever held important office in the American Anti-Slavery Society. As traveling agents of abolition, black speakers were denied seats inside a stage coach or in the cabin of a river steamer and had to ride outside, even in rain or freezing weather. Usually there was no place for them to sleep, except in the house of another black. Generally, they lived in daily fear of their lives.

As the abolition movement gained momentum by the middle of the nineteenth century, blacks had become prominent as speakers, agents, and officials of many organizations. They were the publishers of at least seventeen abolitionist newspapers or journals. And though there were fewer blacks than whites in the organizations that made up the abolition movement, they were more militant than the whites in working for the freedom of their enslaved people.

But black abolitionism took the form of more than just antislavery groups. Blacks moved to strengthen the abolitionist cause by undertaking programs of self-improvement, so as to disprove the charge of racial inferiority. The small black communities in northern cities were closely knit. They banded together to form churches, libraries, literary organizations, temperance societies, committees to aid runaway slaves, and schools. Especially schools, for in 1827 there were only ten schools for blacks in the North. The blacks also cared for one another in illness and misfortune and helped to find and expand job opportunities. And they worked to bolster race pride, to increase their confidence as they demanded the emancipation from slavery they wanted so desperately to bring about. "I thank our Father," wrote Junius C. Morel, a black intellectual, "that it has pleased Him in His wisdom to order our color just as He has."

VII

WOMEN and ABOLITION

At the time the abolition movement began, women as well as blacks were denied freedom and equality. Women could not vote or hold office, and married women could not control their own property. A woman who had to support herself might teach young children if she were sufficiently educated, otherwise almost the only occupations open to her were as seamstress, milliner, or domestic servant. Later, the New England cotton mills began to turn to young women as a source of cheap and easily controlled labor. But almost no college would accept women; and almost no woman could think of being a doctor, lawyer, or public official, or of working in an office. Women were not supposed even to discuss politics or public issues with men and certainly not to speak publicly to audiences that included men. So it was perhaps natural that women, moved by their own lack of freedom, were sensitive to the enslavement of blacks.

The churches were particularly insistent that women maintain a modest silence about controversial public issues. The one exception was the Quaker faith. Women were full members of its meetings, free to speak as the spirit moved them. Though the Quakers had no formal priesthood, women as well as men could be ordained as "ministers" and thereafter would bear a special responsibility as leaders and counsellors. Quakers took the lead in seeking equal rights for women as well as for blacks.

Lucretia Mott was a Quaker, born on Nantucket Island in 1793. The men of Nantucket, including her father, Thomas Coffin, spent months at a time at sea hunting whales, for Nantucket was a center of the whaling industry. During those long months their wives had to manage the families and farms. Many of them, including Lucretia's mother, ran small stores to sell necessities to their neighbors. Women brought up on Nantucket became used to being active and independent people.

Thomas Coffin prospered, and when his daughter was eleven he left the sea, moved his family to Boston, and set up in business as a merchant. After a year or two in a Boston school, Lucretia was sent at thirteen to an excellent Quaker school near Poughkeepsie, New York, where she received a far better education than was usually available, especially for young women. She was an outstanding student, and when she was fifteen she was made an assistant teacher, a position she filled while she completed the last two years of her schooling.

Meanwhile, her parents had moved to Philadelphia, the center of the Quaker faith in America. It was to Philadelphia that Lucretia Coffin came when she finished school in 1810. She was followed by James Mott, a young Quaker who was assistant principal of the school; he had fallen in love with his most promising student. They were married in 1811, when Lucretia was eighteen; and James became a partner in her father's business.

The War of 1812 closed Philadelphia and other American ports to most trade. The new firm of Coffin and Mott went out of business, and for several years the young couple faced hard times. Lucretia Mott taught in a Quaker school to help provide an income for the family. When prosperity returned with the end of the war in 1815, James's business began to flourish. For the rest of their lives, the Motts remained well off.

Lucretia Mott was a woman of great strength and energy. As her three children grew older she began to devote time to affairs outside the home. At first her interest was confined to the Quaker faith. At least as early as 1818, when she was twenty-five, she began to speak at the Sabbath meetings. Three years later she was made a minister.

There was growing tension within the Society of Friends in the 1820s. Many Quakers who had become wealthy and conservative grew rigid in their religious views. They called themselves Orthodox

Friends. Others, inspired by the Quaker leader Elias Hicks, wanted to return to a simpler, more devoted life; they were more liberal in their religious beliefs. The differences grew so great that in 1827 the Quakers divided into two separate groups, the Orthodox Friends and the Hicksite Friends. The Motts were Hicksites. Though she was to remain a devout Quaker throughout her life, Mrs. Mott always opposed efforts to force Quakers into fixed beliefs and practices. A great deal of bitterness arose in the split, but she was able to maintain warm relations with Quakers of both groups.

Elias Hicks had been an early and vigorous opponent of slavery. Mott herself had seen something of its evils when she had journeyed to Quaker meetings in Virginia. The Motts joined the abolition movement. They had been much impressed by Garrison's writings in *The Liberator* and they, too, came to oppose the colonization movement and to insist on immediate emancipation. Mott remained devoted to her home and family, remained active in religious affairs, and took a leading part in the struggle for women's rights. But nothing was more important to her than the battle for the liberation of blacks.

Mott was very enthusiastic about the 1833 convention in Philadelphia that had been called to organize the American Anti-Slavery Society. As a woman, though, she could attend only as an observer, not as a member. She did not let this silence her. When the time came to draw up a declaration of the convention's views, she rose from the observers' section and offered a suggestion that the convention accepted even over the opposition of William Lloyd Garrison himself. The convention went on to decide that women's antislavery organizations should be formed; Mott took immediate steps to organize one in Philadelphia and became its first president. She was an especially effective speaker, for the sweetness of her personality and her obvious goodwill enabled her to state very strong views without turning away her listeners.

Mott made a special effort to persuade whites to stop purchasing the products of slave labor. Her husband had already banned them from his business. She refused to buy or wear anything made of slave-grown cotton or to allow slave-produced sugar in her house.

She also worked with leaders of the black community to improve the condition of free Negroes in Philadelphia. A number of black women were charter members of the Philadelphia Female Anti-Slavery Society. One of them, Sarah Douglas, founded a school for black children that Mott helped to support. In this she was joined by the daughters of James Forten. They became good friends of the Motts and were often in each other's homes.

James Mott became one of the founders of the Pennsylvania Anti-Slavery Society. As soon as women were admitted to membership in it, Lucretia, too, became one of its leaders and served on its executive committee. She was one of the first women in the United States to become an officer of an organization that included both men and women.

She became one of the leaders, in 1837, in forming a national women's antislavery organization. It was at the first annual meeting of that organization in Philadelphia in 1838 that Pennsylvania Hall was burned, destroying all of Benjamin Lundy's property. During the riots at that time, Mott was a strong, cool force. She refused to let the convention be broken up.

In 1840 the American Anti-Slavery Society, convening in New York, fought over the issue of whether women should be addmitted as members. Garrison led the fight for open membership. He chartered a ship, filled it with delegates from Massachusetts, and controlled the meetings. By a narrow vote women were admitted and allowed to hold office. And, following the will of Garrison, the organization became committed to the "women question" among other causes. Lucretia Mott immediately became a leader of the national organization as she was of the Pennsylvania state society. She was picked by the American Anti-Slavery as a delegate to the World Anti-Slavery Convention which was to meet in London, England, in 1840.

Three other women, representing other antislavery organizations, also went to London as delegates. When they arrived in London, they found that the British committee that had organized the convention refused to accept women as members. Most of the American delegates supported the right of the women to be seated, but the convention voted against them. With the other women, Mott sat in the balcony as an observer, as she had done seven years earlier at the founding of the American Anti-Slavery Society. Some of the men among the American delegation, including William Lloyd Garrison and Wendell Phillips, whose wife, Anne, was one of the delegates, refused their seats and joined the women in the balcony. Even from the balcony, though, Mott made her influence felt at the convention.

After her return to America, Mott continued her quiet but vigorous participation in the antislavery movement. The experience of being excluded from the London convention, however, turned her mind more and more to questions of women's rights and women's role in society.

Two other remarkable women who became leaders of abolition were the Grimké sisters, Sarah and Angelina. They were from Charleston, South Carolina, the daughters of a distinguished judge in a prominent slaveholding family. From childhood they had opposed slavery and had taught their black maids to read and write, which was against the law. When their parents died and left them money of their own, they moved to Philadelphia, where they would be freer to oppose slavery. There they both became Quakers.

The Grimké sisters first attracted attention in the antislavery movement in 1835. Following the Boston riots of that year, Angelina wrote a powerful letter to William Lloyd Garrison. She expressed her outrage at the attack that nearly cost him his life and she very eloquently set fourth her support of his principles. Garrison published her letter and it made her well known.

At the time, both sisters were at work on books intended for their fellow Southerners. Angelina's was called *Appeal to the Christian Women of the South;* Sarah's, *Epistle to the Clergy of the Southern States*. Both were published in 1836 and were widely distributed and read. Angelina's, which was especially effective, declared that slavery was wrong in every way, that anyone who bought, sold, or owned slaves was as evil as the slave traders whom most Southerners held in contempt. Since many defenses offered for slavery were based on claims that it was recognized and approved in the Bible, Angelina Grimké devoted much of her book to showing that slavery was opposed to Christian principles and to everything Jesus had taught.

The special emphasis of the book, however, was on the particular responsibility of women in abolishing slavery. From the Bible and from history it gave examples of women who had played an important role in public life. And it pointed out that slavery was not only a public issue. Slavery, said Angelina Grimké, was a moral and religious issue that directly affected the home and the family, which were the special province of women.

Angelina Grimké in her writings argued for full equality for blacks as well as for an end to slavery. She asked, "What man or woman of common sense now doubts the intellectual capacity of the colored people? Who does not know, that with all our efforts as a nation to crush and annihilate the minds of this portion of our race, we have never yet been able to do it?"

While Angelina wrote primarily for southern women, Sarah wrote for southern ministers. Like Angelina, she blasted the idea that the Bible suports slavery and she emphasized the religious duty of all Christian ministers to oppose slavery.

In 1836 Angelina Grimké, who was the better speaker of the sisters, was made an agent of the American Anti-Slavery Society. Like the other agents, she was trained in public speaking by Theodore Weld. For two years she traveled about the country giving antislavery lectures. She took no salary and paid her own expenses. She endured bitter attacks on her by people who were shocked by the very thought of a woman traveling about the country speaking to audiences of both sexes.

She and Theodore Weld were drawn together in their fight for their common cause, and in 1838 they were married. Weld had always been so absorbed in his causes he had ignored his personal happiness. But he had been devoted to Angelina almost from the time he met her. After their marriage she limited her public role, preferring to stand by Weld's side, helping him in all his work. After Weld's health had been broken in the fight to establish abolition in the North, he withdrew from active leadership. He and Angelina, with help from Sarah, established a school dedicated to controlling children with love, not with punishment, and to bringing them up with a sense of responsibility for their fellow human beings.

Two other white women who played important roles in the abolition movement were Maria Weston

Chapman and Lydia Maria Child. Chapman was a wealthy, highly educated, and socially prominent Boston woman who was at the center of radical abolition in that city. One of Garrison's personal and financial supporters, she organized ladies' fairs, where needlework, homemade foods, and other objects were sold to raise money for the cause. She edited a yearly book, *The Liberty Bell*, in which antislavery essays, stories, sermons, and poems were published.

Lydia Maria Child was an editor and writer. She was the author of one of the first important abolitionist books, *An Appeal in Favor of That Class of Americans Called Africans*, published in 1833. She was active in the management of the American Anti-Slavery Society, served on the staff of its official newspaper, *The American Anti-Slavery Standard*, and in 1841 became its editor-in-chief.

Harriet Beecher Stowe was probably the most famous and the most effective of the women who wrote against slavery. She was one of several children of Henry Beecher, a minister who had been president of Lane Institute in Cincinnati when Theodore Weld and his fellow students had their great debate and came out for abolition. President Beecher deplored slavery, but thought it very unfitting for students preparing for the ministry to debate so controversial an issue in such a public way. Harriet's sister Catherine detested slavery too, but she thought it unwomanly to speak in public against it, as had Angelina Grimké, and she thought it unChristian to use such harsh language against slaveowners, most of whom, she believed, were religious men and women who deserved sympathy rather than blame for their problem. Their brother Henry Ward Beecher was to be the most famous minister of his day, serving God with a controlled passion like his father's and sister Catherine's.

But Harriet married a young abolitionist professor named Calvin Stowe; and as Harriet Beecher Stowe she wrote a book, a sentimental melodrama called *Uncle Tom's Cabin,* which became probably the most popular book ever published in the United States. It told the story of a saintly old slave, Uncle Tom; a wicked overseer, Simon Legree; a charming black child, Topsy; an angelic white child, little Eva; and a young, light-skinned man and wife among the slaves, George and Eliza, who made their way to freedom after Eliza escaped the slave-catcher's bloodhounds by leaping from one cake of ice to another across the frozen Ohio River. The book was so widely read that to this day the names of its characters remain part of our language; we still say a child has grown like Topsy and call someone an Uncle Tom or a Simon Legree.

Uncle Tom's Cabin, published in 1852, displeased many abolitionists because, while it showed slavery to be a cruel, inhuman system, and condemned the southern civilization based on it, the book seemed to fall short of thoroughly attacking all aspects of slavery and all slaveowners. But it displeased Southerners even more, as edition after edition poured from the printing presses: three hundred thousand in the first year alone. Traveling companies performed it as a play in tent shows across the country.

Abraham Lincoln, when he first met Harriet Beecher Stowe during the Civil War, greeted her as "the little lady who started it all." And indeed it is not too much to say that *Uncle Tom's Cabin* was the most powerful single force in creating throughout the North the conviction that slavery was a monstrous evil whose spread had to be stopped.

The fight that women had made for the rights of blacks became a fight for the rights of women as well. Women who had spoken to hostile crowds, edited newspapers, petitioned legislatures, organized and chaired meetings, and served on the executive committees of national organizations demanded the chance to play a full part in other aspects of national life. In Seneca Falls, New York, in 1848, a national meeting was held to form an organization to fight for all rights for women, including the right to vote.

It was the beginning of the women's movement in the United States. And almost every one of the leaders at Seneca Falls had proved herself in the antislavery struggle: Lucretia Mott, Elizabeth Cady Stanton, Lucy Stone, Susan B. Anthony, and many others. Rights for women came more slowly than rights for blacks. After the Constitution was amended in 1870 to provide that the right to vote could not be denied because of race, a half-century passed before another amendment provided that the vote could not be denied because of one's sex. But it was in the fight for the liberation of blacks that the fight for the equality of women was begun.

VIII

The GREAT SPLIT

AFTER Garrison and his shipload of delegates from Massachusetts captured control of the American Anti-Slavery Society in 1840, many leading abolitionists left the organization. The members who resigned included such leaders as James G. Birney, Arthur and Benjamin Tappan, and Theodore and Angelina Grimké Weld. They had expected that Garrison might win. The newspaper published by the society, *The Emancipator*, had already been transferred to the New York Anti-Slavery Society, which was firmly controlled by the Tappans and their friends. Those who resigned formed a new organization, The American and Foreign Anti-Slavery Society, which drew its strength from New York and the Midwest. Garrison had won only an empty name. All that was left of the old American Anti-Slavery Society when he took it over was the loyal band of his own followers, most of whom were already members of the Massachusetts Anti-Slavery Society.

The specific issue on which the split came was the right of women to speak, vote, and hold office in the society. But there were other deeper differences between Garrison and his followers and Birney, the Tappans, the Welds, and their allies. Garrison was driven by the idea that men and women could approach perfection in their lives. It was, he was convinced, the duty of all human beings to live by Christ's commands in all aspects of their lives, without making the slightest compromise. He believed that Christianity demanded complete equality for everyone, blacks and whites, women and men. And he believed that any use of force toward another human being was sinful, even if the force were used in a good cause or in self-defense.

These beliefs led Garrison to support many causes in addition to abolition. He was a leader in the pacifist movement, a founder of the American Non-Resistance Society, whose members opposed all wars and criticized Elijah Lovejoy, the editor who was killed by the antiabolitionist mob in Illinois, because he had taken arms to defend himself and his press.

Garrison condemned the national church organizations for not expelling the southern churches that included slaveowners among their members. When the northern churches, upset by the harsh, uncharitable words of the abolitionists, closed their doors to

Garrison's followers, he accused them of sharing the sin of slavery.

The attitude of Garrison toward the churches was vigorously set forth in 1844 by one of his followers, Stephen S. Foster, in a pamphlet, *The Brotherhood of Thieves; or, a True Picture of the American Church and Clergy*. In it he said:

> . . . that the American church and clergy, as a body, were thieves, adulterers, man stealers, pirates and murderers; that the Methodist Episcopal Church was more corrupt and profligate than any house of ill fame in the city of New York; that the southern ministers were desirous of perpetuating slavery for the purpose of supplying themselves with concubines from among the hapless victims and that many of our clergymen were guilty of enormities that would disgrace an Algerine pirate!!

Garrison felt even more bitter about organized government than about organized religion. Eventually he concluded that it was sinful to recognize or take any part—even by voting—in a government that recognized and tolerated slavery.

Many abolitionists had great respect for their churches and for the Union and the Constitution. They were moderate in speech and offended by the language of Garrison and his followers from New England. Though some of them shared Garrison's views on the equality of women, they were unwilling to allow the issue to take attention away from slavery. They wanted not only to denounce slavery, but to use all the practical means they could to confine and reduce it and finally to end it. This not only meant that they would vote, it meant that they would take an active role in politics and try to gain power in government.

In New England, Garrison's American Anti-Slavery Society gained strength—and some important new recruits. One was Wendell Phillips, a brilliant, handsome lawyer from one of the oldest, wealthiest, and most prominent families in Boston. His father had been the city's first mayor. Young Wendell could easily have won great wealth and become one of the leaders of the bar and of business and politics in Massachusetts. Instead, he gave up all these prospects and threw himself into the antislavery movement. He had been moved by Garrison's writings and speeches and also by the efforts to silence the abolitionists. He thought such attempts at censorship threatened the freedom of all Americans.

In September 1837, at a meeting in Boston called to protest the killing of Lovejoy, Phillips had been horrified to hear the attorney general of Massachusetts say that Lovejoy himself was to blame for the riot and that the rioters who killed him were trying to put down evil, in the tradition of the leaders of the Boston Tea Party. Phillips, outraged, rose from his seat and made a fiery speech. He identified the antislavery movement with the finest traditions of New England during the American Revolution.

From that moment Phillips was marked as the most powerful orator in the abolitionist cause. For a quarter of a century he toured the country, lecturing on the evils of slavery and demanding freedom and equality for blacks. He was also in great demand to speak on other subjects. In the 1840s and 1850s popular lectures filled the place that television, movies, and other forms of entertainment do today. Even in small towns, audiences of hundreds would come to hear talks on history, on philosophy, or on foreign countries or public issues.

Phillips became one of the most popular of these lecturers. Even ardent opponents of the antislavery movement thronged to hear him speak on other topics. From these lectures he earned extra money to put into the abolitionist cause. And, once he had won a big audience in some town with a popular lecture, he would follow up with a free antislavery talk.

Though they were later to drift apart, Phillips and Garrison were for many years close friends as well as allies. Garrison named one of his sons for Phillips; Phillips helped Garrison financially from time to time; and the two families saw much of each other.

In 1844 the American Anti-Slavery Society resolved "That secession from the present United States government is the duty of every abolitionist; since no one can take office, or throw a vote for another to hold office, under the United States Constitution, without violating his anti-slavery principles, and rendering himself an abettor of the slaveholder in his sin." "No union with slaveholders!" became a slogan of the society.

Garrison himself went even farther. He denounced the Constitution as "a covenant with Death and an agreement with Hell." He would climax a speech by taking a copy of the Constitution and burning it before his audience. He urged that the Union be dissolved so that the free states would no longer have any legal connection with slavery. He thought this would help to end slavery because slaves could more easily escape into free territory from which they could not be returned. Also, the military strength of the free states could not be called on to help suppress slave uprisings.

Primarily, Garrison and his followers were interested in their own freedom from any sin of having accepted slavery. With Boston friends, and coworkers such as Wendell Phillips, Maria Weston Chapman, Lucretia Mott, John Greenleaf Whittier, and Lydia Maria Child, they continued up to the outbreak of the Civil War to represent abolition in its purest and most uncompromising form.

The Tappans, Birney, the Welds, and others who resigned from the American Anti-Slavery Society when it fell under Garrison's control pursued a very different course. The American and Foreign Anti-Slavery Society, which they founded, never became strong. It had little connection with the state societies and drifted into inactivity. Finally, in the 1850s, it simply faded away, mainly because this group of abolitionists turned instead to politics as the way to achieve their goals. They were more interested in organizing a political party than an antislavery society.

Since the days of John Woolman a century before, abolitionists had argued against slavery and had appealed to the conscience of slaveowners. For nearly a decade *The Liberator* had thundered at the enemies of freedom. Dozens of speakers supported by the American Anti-Slavery Society and trained by Theodore Weld had brought the abolitionist message to every corner of the free states. Congress had been bombarded with petitions bearing hundreds of thousands of signatures. Yet, slavery had spread across the nation and Southerners were defending it more desperately than ever before.

None of this would change, Birney, the Tappans, and their friends came to believe, until the abolitionists got political power. In 1840, with the support of Frederick Douglass, they formed the Liberty party, and nominated Birney for president. Of course he stood no chance of being elected. The abolitionists did not hope for that. But the campaign itself, they thought, would bring the antislavery message to the people. Here and there an antislavery member of Congress might be elected. And from this beginning a strong party might grow in time, gaining in strength from election to election.

Birney won only seven thousand votes, one voter out of every three hundred who went to the polls. But in two states, New York and Maine, the Liberty party got nearly enough votes to hold the balance of power between the evenly balanced Whig and Democratic parties.

The Liberty party members were not discouraged. Their effort in 1840 had been made with little time to prepare. In 1844 the Liberty party once more nominated Birney and drew up a broader platform, denouncing slavery and condemning the annexation of Texas. Their immediate objective was to end slavery in the District of Columbia and put a stop to the interstate slave trade.

In the election of 1844 the annexation of Texas and of the Oregon Territory were burning issues. The Democrats nominated James K. Polk and pledged themselves to the immediate annexation of both. The Whigs nominated Henry Clay. Clay and the Whigs were also for western expansion, but a more cautious expansion than the Democrats wanted. Birney and the Liberty party denounced both opponents, though Polk was the least desirable of the candidates. The victory of either would add the enormous area of Texas to the domain of slavery.

This time Birney won sixty-two thousand votes, one in forty—still a pitifully small number. In three states, though—New York, Ohio, and Michigan—the Liberty party now actually held the balance of power. In New York, Birney drew fifteen thousand votes, most of them from the Whigs. This was enough to let the Democrats carry New York, and it made Polk the president. Polk moved quickly to annex Texas, an action that led to war with Mexico.

This outcome of the election made the Liberty party seem as ineffective as the other abolitionist efforts to end slavery. The federal government ended up in the hands of southern slaveholders and their northern friends, who were determined not only to protect and defend slavery but to expand it. No one then could have guessed that in little more than twenty years slavery, now triumphant, would be completely abolished throughout the United States. And yet it was the victory of Polk and the Democrats that led, eventually, to the Civil War and the abolition of slavery.

IX

SLAVERY and the WEST

IMMEDIATELY after President Polk took office in 1845 Congress voted to annex Texas. It would join the Union as one huge state, but could divide itself into as many as five states if it chose to do so. Texas was an enormous addition to slave territory. The antislavery forces now saw that there might be not only two additional proslavery senators, but as many as ten if Texas should divide itself.

Texas had once been a part of Mexico; the United States not only annexed it, but insisted that the new state stretched as far west as the Rio Grande River. Mexico claimed some of this territory as its own, and this led the United States to go to war, in 1846, with its large but weak neighbor. Antislavery leaders saw the war as one more violent effort of what they called the Slave Power to add territory for slavery.

Many other Americans joined them in denouncing the war as an unjustified attack on Mexico, with no cause but the greedy demand for more and more land.

As the Mexican War went on, antislavery leaders moved to strengthen the Liberty party so that it could be a force against the spread of slavery. A year before the election of 1848, the party nominated John Hale of New Hampshire for president.

In 1848 Mexico was defeated. The American victory not only confirmed the annexation of Texas, but won for the United States a vast new territory stretching to the Pacific. The Missouri Compromise of 1820, which had established a boundary between slavery and freedom in the western territories the United States held at that time, did not apply to this newly acquired empire. Would these new lands be free or would they be a new domain for slavery? For the next twelve years the great issue before the abolition movement was not whether slavery would be abolished in the South, but whether it would be extended to the West.

In the United States Congress, David R. Wilmot, a representative from Pennsylvania, introduced legislation providing that slavery would not be permitted in any of the territory taken from Mexico. Twice his "Proviso," as it was called, passed the House—the first victory antislavery forces had won in Congress since the abolition of the foreign slave trade in 1807. Each time, though, the Senate refused to pass it. It was obvious that the president and the Congress to be elected in 1848 would have to determine whether the new empire in the West would be slave or free.

The Whig party nominated a hero of the Mexican War, General Zachary Taylor, for president. Taylor owned large plantations and more than one hundred slaves in Louisiana and Mississippi, but he had never had anything to say about the expansion of slavery. The Democrats nominated Lewis Cass, a Northerner who did not care whether slavery expanded or not. His view on the new territories was that their settlers should be free to decide whether slavery would be permitted.

Neither of the regular parties offered any hope of excluding slavery from the West, and the Liberty party alone was too small to have any important effect on the decision. But then a new opportunity came. Martin Van Buren, who had been president from 1837 to 1841, condemned the expansion of slavery and decided to leave the Democratic party to run as an independent in 1848. His most loyal followers were small farmers from upstate New York, who wanted the West for themselves, not for the slaveowning southern planters against whom they could not compete. So when Van Buren announced he was running for president, it was on the basis of "free-soil"—a demand that slavery be kept out of the western territories.

The Liberty party withdrew Hale's nomination, joined with other free-soilers opposed to slavery in the West, formed the Free-Soil party, and nominated Van Buren for president. The free-soilers were by no means abolitionists, though. Most of them were willing to leave slavery in the states where it existed. Most did not like blacks; in fact, they supported free-soil so they could keep blacks out of the West. Van Buren himself had never been an opponent of slavery when he was in office. But in the crisis, abolitionists were willing to join with others of very different views if together they could keep slavery out of the new territories.

Van Buren ran a far stronger race than had Birney in 1840 and 1844, receiving about three hundred thousand votes. He did not carry any state, but in several he came in second, ahead of one of the two major candidates. In New York State he took enough votes away from Cass to enable Taylor to win the state—which put Taylor in the White House. The abolitionists had again managed to elect a slave-owning southern president. But, as part of the Free-Soil party, the abolitionists had forced the country to face the slavery issue, which most Americans would have preferred to forget. And they had made it more difficult for an openly proslavery candidate to run successfully in the northern states.

When the new Congress convened in 1849, it had to face the question of the West. California was already seeking admission to the Union as a free state. The presence of slavery in the District of Columbia was a constant and irritating issue. And Southerners were angry about the failure of northern states to return runaway slaves.

Finally, the Senate, led by Henry Clay and Stephen A. Douglas, put together a compromise, the Compromise of 1850. California would be admitted as a free state. The rest of the area won from Mexico would be slave territories or free as their settlers decided. The slave trade, but not slavery itself, would be abolished in the District of Columbia. Under a new, strict, fugitive slave law, the federal government would force the return of runaway slaves. Though California would be a free state, the Compromise would open all the rest of the immense new western empire to the possibility of slavery.

Nevertheless, the Compromise was opposed by the more militant Southerners, led by Jefferson Davis and John C. Calhoun, who demanded protection for slavery everywhere—in the District of Columbia and all the territories. President Taylor grew angry with the stubborn Southerners and stopped supporting the Compromise. It was opposed as well by antislavery men and women throughout the North. Then, Calhoun and Taylor died. The new president, Millard Fillmore, supported the Compromise, and Senator Douglas managed to push the Compromise of 1850 to passage.

Most Americans now hoped that the slavery issue was settled. Almost everyone conceded that each state had the right to control the existence of slavery within its own borders. It was thought that the Fugitive Slave Act of 1850 might settle the last major southern grievance. Now perhaps the country could turn from this divisive issue to the joyous prospect of developing the West.

This time of quiet did not come. One reason was that the Fugitive Slave Act brought the horror of slavery home to the North. Fugitive slaves who had lived long and peacefully in northern cities were seized by slave-catchers and dragged in chains through the streets of New York and Boston, to be placed on ships carrying them back to slavery.

For many years there had been efforts to capture runaway slaves and return them to their owners. One case, in 1839, involved a group of slaves led by a powerful black named Cinqué. They seized and killed the Captain of the *Amistad,* a small Spanish ship carrying them to slavery in the West Indies, demanding that the crew bring them back to Africa. But at night, when Cinqué and his followers could not tell the direction by the sun, the crew sailed westward toward America. The ship landed on Long Island and the blacks were imprisoned. They would have been turned over to the Spanish government to be tried for piracy and murder if Benjamin Tappan had not provided money for their defense. Their defenders claimed that the Africans had been illegally enslaved by the Spanish, that they had a right to free themselves, and that they were free men who should be returned to their homes in Africa. The United States government itself wanted to turn the men over to Spain and had a ship ready to take them, but a judge ordered them freed. The case was appealed to the United States Supreme Court, where John Quincy Adams himself argued for their freedom. The Supreme Court agreed that the men should be free, and they were at last brought back to Africa.

This was only the most dramatic of many legal struggles on northern soil to hand blacks over to slavery. For years the Underground Railroad had been carrying thousands of slaves to freedom in the North and in Canada.

Perhaps as many as one hundred thousand men and women had escaped slavery in this way. Daring men and women in the northern states or in the upper South smuggled slaves to the Ohio River or to the Pennsylvania border. Harriet Tubman, the black abolitionist and former slave, was the most famous, but there were others as daring. John Fairfield was a Virginia white man whose own family held slaves, but he dedicated his life to the Underground Railroad. Again and again he went through the South, pretending to be a traveling merchant or a slave trader himself. With his southern speech and manners, he could avoid suspicion and organize small bands of blacks for escape. He continued through the years until he was killed in 1860. Others, black and white, like Josiah Henson or John Mason ran equal risks, and some, like Elijah Anderson, died in prison.

Once blacks got to northern cities, they felt fairly safe before 1850. Local "Vigilance Committees" would help them to conceal their identities and get jobs and homes. Efforts were made from time to time to arrest former slaves and return them to their former owners; but the same Vigilance Committees gave warning and help. Even so, thousands of fugitives did not feel safe in the northern United States and made their way to Canada.

Under the Fugitive Slave Act passed in 1793, slaveholders were not often successful in recapturing the men and women they claimed to own. The

Fugitive Slave Act of 1850 was designed to make it much easier to recapture an escaped slave. Anyone who said he owned a slave or represented an owner could seize any black he claimed to own. If he could produce satisfactory evidence of ownership, he could bring the black to a slave state. The person seized could not testify in his or her own behalf and no state court or official could interfere. Black men and women who were born free, who might never have set foot in a slave state, were placed in great danger. The law left them defenseless if a slave-catcher came up with documents, however false, that seemed to show ownership.

Many Northerners who were by no means abolitionists were shocked. They were willing to leave slavery alone in the South if whites there wanted it. But they were horrified at slavery's reaching into their own towns with chains and manacles. In Boston, leading citizens organized committees to defy the new Fugitive Slave Act and protect the blacks of their city. Southerners became increasingly angry as northerners defied the Fugitive Slave Act by passing personal-liberty laws, aiding blacks in state courts, and even rescuing blacks from slave-catchers. After *Uncle Tom's Cabin* was published in 1852, the South almost exploded in rage. Though there were still only a few thousand true abolitionists who were determined to end slavery throughout the country, there were now hundreds of thousands who were convinced that the spread of slavery had to be stopped.

The Compromise of 1850, and especially the Fugitive Slave Act, became the major issue of the 1852 presidential election. The Free-Soil party, condemning the Compromise, this time ran John Hale. The Whigs, agreeing reluctantly with the Compromise, but more concerned about avoiding division and promoting economic growth, chose General Winfield Scott. The Democrats, proslavery and pro-South, nominated Franklin Pierce, "a northern man with southern principles," who supported the Fugitive Slave Act and was willing to leave slavery undisturbed. He was elected overwhelmingly: by the South because to Southerners the Whigs were not enthusiastic enough about slavery; by the North because northern whites were more disgusted with the slavery controversy than they were with slavery. Though many Northerners were sickened by the Fugitive Slave Act, Americans in general wanted to be left alone to develop their big, young land. They did not especially like blacks and had no wish to break up the Union for the benefit of some slaves. In fact, though there was of course no slavery in the North, blacks were not even given the right to vote in the new, free territories that entered the Union.

In spite of the Compromise of 1850, the issue of whether slavery would spread to the expanding West soon arose again. Settlers began to pour across the Missouri River into the territories north of what is now Oklahoma. Soon these territories would have to be granted organized territorial government.

The Missouri Compromise of 1820 had barred slavery from all the Louisiana Purchase territory north of the southern boundary of Missouri. Senator

Stephen A. Douglas of Illinois wanted to open the territories west of Missouri to settlement; he also wanted southern support for a railroad route that would go across the central part of the continent. Douglas introduced a bill to the Congress in 1854 that established territories, Kansas and Nebraska, and would let the legislature in each decide if it would be free or slave. In effect, this meant that Nebraska would be free and Kansas possibly slave, which ignored the Missouri Compromise. Douglas hoped the Kansas-Nebraska Act would appeal to everyone. Westerners would be glad to see the new lands opened up. Southerners would welcome the idea that the federal government would allow slavery the right to expand wherever the white voters wanted it to. And the day would be nearer when a railroad could be built from Chicago to California.

Douglas was dead wrong. Though people in the North were willing to leave slavery undisturbed in the slave states, they wanted it to spread no farther. Now that the Missouri Compromise was being abandoned, the whole West might be infested with slavery. People who cared little about blacks were outraged to think that farm lands they wanted for themselves might come to be owned not by free men working their fields themselves but by the wealthy planters using slave labor.

Slaveowners made no effort to take over the Nebraska Territory, but moved west over the borders of Missouri to try to establish their control over Kansas. New England abolitionist groups raised money to aid migrants who would help make Kansas free. Both proslavery and antislavery settlers came armed. There were bloody fights and midnight raids back and forth among the primitive settlements. Two separate territorial governments were set up, one slave and one free, each with its own crude capital. The territorial governor appointed by President Pierce favored the proslavery government, which was officially recognized though it represented only a minority of the people.

In the midst of this struggle came the election of 1856. The Democrats chose James Buchanan, an elderly bachelor from Pennsylvania. Buchanan had been the American ambassador in London during the Kansas-Nebraska struggle, so he had not had to take sides or make enemies. In general he supported the Kansas-Nebraska and Fugitive Slave Acts, but hoped to turn the country's mind from slavery to other issues.

After its dismal showing in 1852, the Whig party had all but disappeared. Many of the more conservative Whigs, who also did not want to see the country further torn by the slavery issue, joined a new party called the American party. It was also known as the Know-Nothing party, for its main purpose was to oppose the new immigrants, largely Irish Catholic and German, who were swarming into the cities; but the Whigs who entered it hoped to give it a broader base. They nominated Millard Fillmore, the former president who had signed the Compromise of 1850.

Neither of these parties met the need of the growing numbers of voters who were determined that slavery should not spread. In the Congressional elections of 1854 the Democrats had lost heavily in the North. Their opponents were not yet united; they ran under many party labels. But within the next year these various groups—including old Liberty and Free-Soil party members, antislavery Whigs, and many northern Democrats—opposed to the spread of slavery, came together to form the Republican party. By 1856 it was well established and ready to enter the election in all the northern states.

For president the Republicans nominated John C. Frémont, a dashing young army officer who had no political experience but who had become famous as an explorer of the West. Behind him were almost all those who had been fighting politically for the abolition of slavery. Their short platform proclaimed once more the unalienable right of all men to life, liberty, and the pursuit of happiness, and denied the right of Congress to permit slavery in any territory. They were particularly opposed to the effort to plant slavery in Kansas, and demanded Kansas's immediate admission as a free state.

The Republicans campaigned vigorously. Their meetings were like religious revivals, with bands and torchlight parades. Antislavery leaders like Wendell Phillips, Ralph Waldo Emerson, and Senator John Hale toured the country making passionate speeches. The Republicans made no pretense of being a truly national party trying to bring North and South together by ignoring or somehow compromising the slavery issue. They were proudly antislavery and made no effort to appeal to the South.

Threats from the South to secede from the Union to form a separate nation frightened many Northerners into voting for the Democrats. Buchanan was elected, but he received only forty-five percent of the votes, and the Republicans won in most of the free states. For the first time, the antislavery forces were the leading political party in the North, and North and South were sharply split.

Still, the Democrats, friendly to slavery and dedicated to holding the Union together, had won again. Buchanan spent his four years in the presidency trying to keep the divisive issue quiet. But that was impossible. Southern leaders were now demanding not only that slavery be protected within the slave states, but that it have the right to exist in every territory controlled by the federal government. Beyond that, some Southerners were pressing for further American expansion, into Mexico, Central America, and Cuba, so that slavery would have more room to grow in climates to which plantation agriculture was suited. Some were even demanding that the slave trade be reopened so that fresh supplies of blacks could be brought in to strengthen the institution. Kansas remained in turmoil and two other events rocked the nation. One took place in the quiet courtroom of the United States Supreme Court, one on the bloody heights of Harpers Ferry, Virginia.

The court case involved a slave named Dred Scott. His master had been an army doctor who had brought Scott into the free state of Illinois and then into the northern part of the Louisiana Purchase, where slavery had been prohibited under the Missouri Compromise. Scott sued for his freedom and that of his family, arguing that they had been emancipated by having been brought into free territory. The Supreme Court's opinion, written by Chief Justice Roger Taney, held that blacks, even free ones, were not citizens and had no legal rights. The Court even went further. It held that Congress could not limit the right of a citizen to go into any territory and bring his property with him, even if that property included slaves. This meant that the whole Missouri Compromise was unconstitutional from the beginning, and that every territory acquired by the United States, including the entire West, must be open to slavery.

The decision was a stunning blow not only to opponents of slavery, but to the many Northerners who were uncomfortable with the increasing power of the southern planters. Even if antislavery forces gained control of Congress, the Constitution, as interpreted by the Supreme Court, left them powerless to stop the spread of slavery. And the South, the Slave Power, clearly controlled the nation.

If legal means to limit slavery were futile, it was inevitable that some would turn to violence. John Brown was a somber, intense, white man who believed that God had chosen him to advance the cause of freedom. He had moved with his sons to Kansas, and during the struggle there he and his small band had killed a number of proslavery men. When Kansas quieted down he returned to the East and began to form a scheme to invade the South to free as many slaves as possible. He tried to convince abolitionist leaders like Douglass, Garrison, Weld, and Phillips to join him, but none would.

Brown's plan was to seize the lightly guarded United States arsenal at Harpers Ferry. Here he would get weapons to arm the hundreds of slaves he was confident would rise up to join him. Harpers Ferry was surrounded by mountains into which Brown and the newly freed slaves could retreat and carry on guerilla warfare. Here they could welcome other escaped slaves, gather strength, march south, and overthrow the whole monstrous institution of slavery. The Pennsylvania boundary was not far away, and blacks who did not want to stay and fight could be smuggled to freedom.

After dark on October 16, 1859, Brown and his band made a surprise attack on the arsenal and easily captured it. They could have gotten to the mountains without difficulty, but Brown kept them at the arsenal expecting the slaves who would pour in to join him. None did. Soon, local militia and a company of United States Marines under Colonel Robert E. Lee were raining bullets at the arsenal. Brown's men had no chance. Most of them were killed, including two of Brown's sons. Brown was badly wounded, but captured alive. Tried for treason and murder, he was convicted and hanged. He had been a bitter, violent, half-insane old man, but at his trial he behaved with great dignity. He made a moving final statement to the court when he was sentenced. "I am yet too young to understand that God is any respecter of persons," he said. "I believe that to have interfered as I have done—as I have always freely admitted I have done—in behalf of His despised poor, was not wrong, but right. Now, if it is deemed necessary that I should forfeit my life for the furtherance of the ends of justice, and mingle my blood further with the blood of my children and with the blood of millions in this slave country whose rights are disregarded by wicked, cruel, and unjust enactments, I say, let it be done!"

After Brown was hanged, he became a hero to abolitionists, a martyr to the holy battle against slavery. "John Brown's body lies a'mouldering in the grave, but his soul goes marching on!" they sang.

The lines had been drawn. To supporters of abolition, all the doors to the peaceful elimination of slavery seemed closed. All the West had been opened to its spread. The Dred Scott decision put the Constitution itself firmly on the side of slavery. John Brown became a symbol of the need for action, not words.

At the same time, to southern slaveowners John Brown became a symbol of what they had always believed was the abolitionists' willingness to stir up the slaves to slaughter them in their beds. The South gathered arms for the coming battle. With the Dred Scott decision to support them, Southerners were more determined than ever to settle the West as well and to bring slavery with them.

It was no longer possible to confine slavery to the southern states and expect that someday Southerners themselves would do away with it. Slavery would triumph, or it would be ended by force. For half a century Northerners had simply hoped that slavery could be forgotten. Though many disliked the institution, they had hated abolitionists more. Garrison, Phillips, Weld, Douglass, and their allies had never been able to persuade most Northerners to take action against slavery. But they had planted the conviction throughout the free states that it was wrong. Now, a choice had to be made. And John Brown's death convinced thousands to switch to the Republican party. Throughout the North the conviction began to harden. There were nearly four million slaves in the nation. Slavery had to be stopped where it was, Dred Scott decision or no Dred Scott decision. The issue so long compromised and dodged had to be faced.

★X★

WAR and FREEDOM

THE facing of issues came in the election of 1860. The Democratic party was the one remaining political organization that stretched across the entire nation. Stephen A. Douglas seemed the obvious man to be its nominee for president. He was the most widely known political leader in the country. He had sponsored the Kansas-Nebraska Act, which he thought was the best answer to North-South conflict. He could reassure the Southerners that they had the same right as others to go to the territories with all their property, including their slaves. At the same time, he could assure the opponents of slavery that geography and climate would keep slavery from the West even if the law did not. He could plead with his fellow Americans to leave slavery to work out its own future and to turn their attention to the enormous task of developing America, opening its unsettled lands, building a national railroad network, enlarging its cities, constructing its factories, entering their country's golden future.

But such a middle course no longer satisfied the North or the South. Douglas was nominated by the Democrats, but not before most of the southern delegates had walked out of the convention and nominated John Breckinridge of Kentucky as the candidate of the southern defenders of slavery. The remnants of the old Whig and Know-Nothing parties nominated John Bell, a conservative Tennesseean, whose only platform was to preserve the Union.

The real political enthusiasm, however, was found in the new Republican party, which had been growing rapidly since its strong showing in its first national campaign in 1856. In a lively and excited convention the Republicans passed over well-known leaders like William Seward of New York and Salmon P. Chase of Ohio, both outspoken opponents of slavery, to nominate an Illinois lawyer named Abraham Lincoln. Lincoln was a newcomer to national politics. He had served only one term in Congress, as a Whig, from 1847 to 1849, and had run unsuccessfully for the Senate against Douglas in 1858.

Lincoln's position on slavery was very clear. He was willing to admit that the Constitution allowed the individual states to permit slavery within their boundaries and he had no intention of trying to force them to abolish it. But he was against its expansion. And there was no doubt how he felt about the institution itself. He had said, "Now, I confess myself as belonging to the class in the country who contemplates slavery as a moral, social, and political evil, having due regard for its actual existence among us and the difficulties of getting rid of it in any satisfactory way, and to all the constitutional obligations which have been thrown about it; but nevertheless, [I] desire a policy that looks to the prevention of it as a wrong, and looks hopefully to the time when as a wrong it may come to an end." For the first time a major candidate for the presidency had dedicated himself to the ultimate elimination of slavery.

Abolitionists were not unanimous in their support of Lincoln, for he was far from an abolitionist himself. For all his hatred of slavery, he put the Constitution and the Union first. He pledged himself not to interfere with slavery in the states. Nor did he believe that blacks were really the equal of whites, or that blacks and whites could successfully live together as equals. Republican speakers said over and over again that slaveholders were not threatened by the Republican party anywhere that slavery already existed.

Such positions disgusted the sterner abolitionists. A handful of them formed the Radical Abolitionist party and nominated Gerrit Smith for president. Men like Frederick Douglass denounced Lincoln and the Republicans for tolerating the continuation of slavery in those states in which it was legal. But most abolitionists, however much they regretted the party's cautious stand, vigorously supported the

Republican candidates. They sensed that a Republican victory would open the path to freedom. Even Garrison, though he still refused to join a political party or vote, urged Lincoln's election.

No candidate got a majority of the popular vote. Lincoln led with about forty percent to Douglas's thirty percent, Breckinridge's seventeen percent, and Bell's thirteen percent. But more important was the way the various regions voted. Except for the divided vote of New Jersey, Lincoln carried every free state and got not one single electoral vote in the ten southern states. Douglas carried only Missouri and part of New Jersey. Bell won the border states of Kentucky, Tennessee, and Virginia. The rest of the South went for Breckinridge. Lincoln had a clear majority of the electoral vote. The nation was now finally divided. Every northern state had voted for a party and candidate pledged to confining slavery immediately and ending it ultimately. Except for a few states bordering on the North, every southern state had voted for a party pledged to the all-out defense of slavery, at the cost of the Union if need be.

Abolitionists, even those who had most savagely criticized Lincoln, rejoiced that he had won. While he was fighting Lincoln's nomination by the Republicans a few months earlier, Wendell Phillips had denounced him as a "Slave-Hound"; but now he saw Lincoln's election as the beginning of the end of slavery.

For all the reassurances given by Lincoln and his fellow Republicans that they would leave slavery undisturbed in the states, Southerners interpreted his election just as the abolitionists had. They now saw the federal government as an enemy of their whole way of life. Even before Lincoln's inauguration, seven states of the deep South, led by South Carolina, seceded from the United States and formed the Confederate States of America. Most Northerners were deeply shocked by this action. Throughout the North the abolitionists were blamed for the destruction of the Union. Their meetings were broken up and their speakers shouted down.

For many years Garrison, Phillips, and many other abolitionists had wanted the Union to break up. Phillips in particular thought that if the Union could get rid of the southern states, it would be freed of the stain of slavery; and Southerners could not maintain slavery without the protection of the federal army. Now he and his fellow radicals had their wish. The slave states, or most of them, were leaving the Union. The abolitionists were determined to offer no compromise to keep them in. It hardly occurred to them that Lincoln would be likely to go to war to force the slave states to remain part of the United States.

But then, on April 15, 1861, Confederate guns fired on Fort Sumter, a United States fort in the harbor of Charleston, South Carolina. War had begun. If the Union was willing to go to battle with the Slave Power, abolitionists would join the fight with a "Hurrah!" And once the South took arms, antiabolitionist Northerners were ready to fight as well.

Even Garrison, who had always opposed all use of force, now supported the Union armies. The last to support the war was Wendell Phillips, but he too was finally caught up in the war fever. Nine days after the attack on Fort Sumter—which he had been willing to give to South Carolina—Phillips gave one of his greatest speeches. To a cheering Boston crowd he went all out for the war. "Years hence," he said, "when the smoke of this conflict clears away, the world will see under one banner all tongues, all creeds, all races—one brotherhood—and on the banks of the Potomac, the Genius of Liberty, robed in light, four and thirty stars in her diadem, broken chains under her feet, and an olive branch in her right hand."

Abolitionists, Republicans, and northern Democrats all supported the war. But they differed widely in what they thought the war was being fought to win. Lincoln was very clear. He was fighting the war to save the Union. Later he was to say: "My paramount object in this struggle *is* to save the Union, and is *not* either to save or destroy slavery. If I could save the Union without freeing *any* slave I would do it, and if I could save it by freeing *all* the slaves I would do it; and if I could save it by freeing some and leaving others alone I would also do that." The abolitionists' goal was the opposite: to end slavery. They—or at least Phillips and Garrison—had been willing to destroy the Union when that seemed to them the best way to attack slavery. Now they were willing to fight for the Union, but only because they now believed a Union victory would mark the end of slavery.

The abolitionists pressed Lincoln hard to announce that the destruction of slavery was a goal of the war, and to free immediately the slaves of any owner who supported the rebellion. He was bombarded with speeches, editorials, and visits from abolitionist leaders. But his immediate concern was to hold in the Union the slave states that had refused to secede—Delaware, Maryland, Kentucky, and Missouri.

Two of his eager generals who were opposed to slavery, Hunter and Frémont, issued orders freeing slaves captured by their forces. Lincoln shocked the abolitionists by reversing their orders. He even continued to enforce the Fugitive Slave Act in the District of Columbia. His only move toward ending slavery was to ask Congress to authorize funds that could be used to repay slaveholders in those loyal states that might free their slaves gradually. He would have been satisfied if such a system provided for the end of slavery by 1900. Even with such a gradual emancipation, Lincoln believed that the freed blacks should find homes outside the United States. He made efforts to set up colonies for them in Central America and elsewhere.

Abolitionists were disillusioned. What was the use of spending lives and fortunes to preserve the Union if the Union was still to be devoted to the protection of slavery? They were willing to fight, but their fight would have to be for freedom. Garrison,

Phillips, and a number of other leading abolitionists across the North in the autumn of 1861 formed an Emancipation League dedicated to making the war one for freedom as well as Union. They worked hard to draw into the fight other leaders who had not been dedicated abolitionists, so as to make emancipation every Northerner's cause. They insisted that blacks be enlisted in the Union armies. They hammered home the argument that freeing the slaves was a military necessity. By letting the millions of slaves know that a Union victory would mean their freedom, the North could win the cooperation of the vast army of blacks whose labor was being used to support the southern cause.

If there were great pressures on Lincoln to proclaim the end of slavery, there were equally strong pressures on him not to do so. Northern whites feared a rush of newly freed blacks from the South would end in mixing the races and would take countless jobs away from white workers. Lincoln also had to worry that Northerners would resent paying for and fighting a war that benefitted blacks more than whites. He felt he had to wait to move until public opinion in the North would support emancipation. Thanks largely to the arguments and efforts of the abolitionists, he was convinced by the late summer of 1862 that the time had come. He drew up an emancipation proclamation, but waited to issue it until a victory in the war could give it more meaning. That victory came in the Battle of Antietam in September. On September 22 a preliminary proclamation was issued. It said that if the rebellion were still in force on January 1, 1863, all slaves in the rebellious states would be forever free. When January 1 came the final Emancipation Proclamation was issued.

In the eyes of the abolitionists it had many shortcomings. It did not apply to the slave states that had remained in the Union. It did not even apply to some areas in Tennessee, Louisiana, and Virginia already conquered by the northern army. It did not, in fact, immediately free any slaves. But the abolitionists and the blacks saw the Proclamation as the great victory it was. Northern victory and black freedom were now linked. Every conquest, every mile the Union army advanced, meant a wider realm for freedom. Slaves throughout the South would know that their liberation depended on the defeat of the Confederate armies, and would do what they dared to bring that day closer. Garrison, who had called Lincoln a man "without moral vision" who might change his mind at the last minute, now called the Proclamation "a great historic event, sublime in its magnitude, momentous and beneficent in its far-reaching consequences."

The Emancipation Proclamation made it certain that slavery would never be restored as it had been before the war. But the task of the abolitionists was by no means over. Emancipation had been decreed by the president alone, as a military necessity under what he claimed as his war powers. But when the war was over and he no longer had such powers, what would the legal situation be? Also the Proclamation did not affect slavery in the loyal states—

Delaware, Maryland, Kentucky, and Missouri. Abolitionists wanted the end of slavery written into the Constitution itself, where it would be effective everywhere and forever, beyond the reach of Congress or of any future president.

Throughout 1863 abolitionists campaigned for an amendment to the Constitution abolishing slavery. They were no longer the outcast radicals of the prewar years. Phillips was one of the most popular speakers in the country, drawing throngs wherever he appeared. Garrison was almost a national hero.

Their leader in the Senate was Charles Sumner, the tall, handsome scholarly Massachusetts lawyer who had already become famous as an antislavery leader before the Civil War. Sumner was not an easy man to like. He was vain and often pompous. He was earnest, humorless, and self-righteous. But he was also hard-working and intelligent and a powerful speaker and writer. In his earlier years he had been an outsider in Washington, ridiculed for his manners and what were then thought his radical ideas. But now most of the country had come around to Sumner's views on Reconstruction. He had become a powerful leader and a hero to the abolitionists and their allies.

The abolitionists now had mass support and real political power. Hundreds of thousands signed petitions for the amendment. In April 1864 the Senate, under Sumner's leadership, voted for an antislavery amendment. The House added its vote in January 1865. Three-fourths of the states had to ratify the amendment before it could become part of the Constitution. But with the southern states out of the Union, this number was reached easily. On December 18, 1865, the Thirteenth Amendment was ratified. It said: "Neither slavery nor involuntary servitude . . . shall exist within the United States, or any place subject to their jurisdiction."

For many abolitionists the long fight was over. Months before, in April 1865, the Confederate armies had surrendered. The Slave Power was crushed and at the mercy of the North. The Constitution itself proclaimed the end of slavery.

William Lloyd Garrison had his moment of triumph even before the last state had ratified the Thirteenth Amendment. He was invited to be a distinguished guest when the United States flag was raised again over Fort Sumter, four years after it had been hauled down under Confederate bombardment. Freedmen, as the emancipated slaves were now called, filled the streets of Charleston in Garrison's honor, and he was carried through crowds on the shoulders of former slaves. What a victory it must have seemed, and in the very heart of what had been the Slave Power! Garrison must have remembered the day, thirty years before, when a very different crowd in his own city of Boston had threatened his life because he had dared to speak out for human freedom. The long years of poverty and abuse, of ridicule and threat, of being stoned and denounced and of having a price placed on his head, of living in grinding poverty—all this now seemed worthwhile. The slaves were free at last. And Garrison himself was a great man, the cheers of thousands ringing in his ears, honored by the very government he had so often reviled.

It is little wonder that Garrison felt the job was done, the final victory won. When the American Anti-Slavery Society held its annual meeting in May 1865, Garrison urged it to disband. It would be "an absurdity," he said, "to maintain an antislavery society after slavery is dead."

★XI★

POSTWAR ABOLITIONISM

THE American Anti-Slavery Society did not disband. Wendell Phillips, Frederick Douglass, and other abolitionist leaders insisted that the society's task was far from done. The nearly four million newly freed slaves, without land or tools or money or education, without the right to vote, with no legal protection, were still helpless before their former masters. Phillips felt that slavery would not be truly ended until blacks and whites were equal before the law and at the ballot box. And he and many other abolitionists were determined to see that blacks had the chance to acquire the land and education they would need to protect their equality. They voted down Garrison's motion to dissolve the society and pledged themselves to continue the fight.

Many conservative whites wanted Congress to pass laws that would force the freedmen to continue to work the farms and plantations of the South. Some even believed these laws were needed to protect helpless blacks. But the abolitionists insisted that blacks were not children; they did not need control or protection, they needed the legal right to manage their own affairs, without any segregation or discrimination.

Under slavery it had been illegal even to teach a black to read. The abolitionists realized that an enormous educational effort was needed if the former slaves were to gain the ability to read and write which they needed to make their way in freedom.

Realistic abolitionists and other friends of the freedmen also knew that as long as all the land in the South remained in the hands of whites, blacks whose only skill was farming would have to go back to working for the owners on whatever terms the whites would offer. The result might not be very different from slavery. But, said the abolitionists, if the large plantations that had been owned by the Confederate rebels could be seized, divided into small farms, and given to the former slaves, it might give them economic independence as well as justly punish the white Southerners for having rebelled.

Even in the North almost every state denied the vote to blacks or imposed requirements on them, such as owning a city lot or other property, that were not imposed on whites. Most abolitionists would have been satisfied with what they called "impartial suffrage," which meant that blacks and whites would be treated alike under the election laws. But the more radical abolitionists wanted universal manhood suffrage. By this they meant that all men would be allowed to vote, whether or not they owned property or could read or anything else. (Almost no one was radical enough to suggest that *any* woman, white or black, rich or poor, should be allowed to vote!) They realized that so long as the ex-slaves were poor and uneducated, property requirements and literacy tests, even if they were applied equally to whites and blacks, would deny the vote to blacks.

One of the first things the abolitionists got Congress to do was to create the Freedmen's Bureau, in March 1865. The bureau provided emergency food and housing and built hospitals for the newly freed slaves. It settled about thirty thousand people on the land, much of it land taken from the former slaveholders. It found jobs for blacks, set up a court system to offer justice to the freedmen, and built thousands of schools. Southern whites hated the bureau; to them it was the government of a foreign power.

The period after the Civil War was called "Reconstruction," a time in which the nation was trying to heal, rebuild, and reunite itself. It could be a time of great promise for blacks, the abolitionists knew. But much depended on how the southern states were readmitted to the Union. Once they became full-fledged members of the Union again, each of the southern states would be able to make its own laws about property, education, voting, and segregation. Each would then be able to do as it pleased with blacks so long as it did not restore slavery. Abolitionists feared that most of the gains won by the war would be lost if the old slaveholding class regained control.

Yet Abraham Lincoln was prepared to see the southern states readmitted on the easiest possible terms. Lincoln announced that as soon as ten percent of the white men in any state had taken an oath of loyalty to the Union, they could elect delegates to a convention to draw up a new constitution for that state. The only requirement was that that constitution should abolish slavery. Then the state could elect senators and representatives and resume its place in the Union. In fact, it would have even more power than it had before the war, when the United States Constitution had provided that only three-fifths of the slaves should be counted in determining how many members of Congress a state would have. Now all the former slaves would be counted, giving almost every southern state one or more additional seats in the House of Representatives, at the expense of the northern states. Abolitionists were outraged: Such a mild policy would give back to the former slaveowners most of the power they had lost in the war.

Abraham Lincoln was assassinated in April 1865, before his policy could be put fully into effect. Abolitionists and their friends hoped that Andrew Johnson, the new president, would pursue a harsher policy. Johnson was a Southerner who hated slave-owners and the power slavery gave them, and had remained loyal to the Union. Charles Sumner and Wendell Phillips thought that Johnson would destroy the old southern slaveholding aristocracy.

But Johnson was more interested in the small white farmers in the South. He did not want to see blacks competing with them for jobs or land or political power. So he continued Lincoln's policies. In most of the southern states the governments that were set up excluded blacks from all political participation. As the abolitionists had feared, these states quickly acted to put the freedmen back into semislavery. They were denied the vote. No provision was made for their education. The state legislatures enacted "Black Codes," which gave blacks far fewer rights than whites and punished them more severely than whites for the same crimes. In several states blacks were required each year to have a contract to work for someone for the full year; if they had no contract, they could be arrested and forced to work for the highest bidder. Mississippi's Black Code forced blacks to remain on the farm by denying them the right to move to towns or, unless they were already town residents, to take jobs there.

Soon, the Republican-controlled Congress was flooded with letters and petitions from furious antislavery Northerners and southern blacks. In response, Republicans in Congress passed the Civil Rights Act of 1866, which said that blacks had the same rights as whites and that anyone who practiced discrimination could be fined or jailed. It also strengthened and extended the life of the Freedmen's Bureau indefinitely. Then, the Republicans proposed the Fourteenth Amendment to the Constitution. It gave citizenship to the ex-slaves and guaranteed that all people in the United States, no matter what their color, were to be treated fairly under the law, even if they had once been slaves. The Fourteenth Amendment did not require that blacks be allowed to vote, though it had a loose, never enforced provision reducing the representation in Congress of states that denied them the vote. Nor did it specifically forbid segregation in schools and other public places. If it had, it would not have gotten much support in Congress, because most Northerners did not think that the freedmen had the education or experience to vote intelligently, and most did not want to be forced to be with blacks, whom they simply did not like.

In the congressional election of 1866 those Republicans who opposed President Johnson won a big victory. The "Radical Republicans," as they called themselves, gained firm control of Congress. They began to pass laws to punish the former Confederates and to protect the rights of the former slaves. In the Senate they were led by Charles Sumner.

The leader of the Radical Republicans in the House of Representatives was Thaddeus Stevens of Pennsylvania. Stevens, a man in his seventies, had a powerful build, a club foot, and a dour and unsmiling face. A hard and grasping man of business who had few close friends, he owned an iron foundry which had made him wealthy. When he spoke on the floor of the House his words were usually bitter. All his life Stevens had shown a deep concern for the poor and those who suffered from discrimination or prejudice. He fought hard for free public schools for everyone in Pennsylvania, which was a radical idea at the time. His will provided that when he died, he should be buried in the black cemetery in his home town. He said that he was unwilling to have his body rest in ground from which men and women were barred because of their race.

Stevens was a zealous Republican, determined to protect his party's control of the government. He hated the southern leaders, whom he saw as proud aristocrats, flaunting the wealth they had won from the labor of men and women held in slavery. Enraged that "they have exchanged forgiveness with the President and been sent on their way rejoicing," he wanted to see at least a few of the rebel leaders hanged.

When the newly elected Congress met in special session in March 1867, no senators or representatives elected by the former Confederate states were seated. The new governments set up in some of these states were abolished, and all of them were put back under military rule. No state was to be allowed back in the Union until a convention had been elected by the votes of all men in the state, black and white, except for some former Confederate leaders, who were not to be allowed to vote. This convention would have to draw up a state constitution that gave the vote to blacks. And it would have to ratify the Fourteenth Amendment.

President Johnson vetoed all the Reconstruction bills, but Congress passed them over his veto. The Union army once more took over the administration of the South. Military government, harsher then before, was reimposed. The constitutional conventions and the legislatures met. Many members of both were blacks. Many others were Northerners who had moved South, sometimes from a sincere desire to help in rebuilding the region, sometimes in the greedy expectation of making money. White Southerners called them all "carpetbaggers." The southern whites who joined the Republican party they called "scalawags."

The new conventions and legislatures changed many things. They repealed all the Black Codes. They provided for public schools for all. They adopted state constitutions that allowed blacks as well as whites to vote. When these newly reorganized state governments applied for readmission to the Union, their senators and representatives were seated.

But the former abolitionist leaders knew that the freedmen were still not adequately protected. Blacks were a majority only in Mississippi and South Carolina. Even in those states the wealthier, better educated, more experienced, and better organized whites might soon regain control. They could then amend their constitutions or pass laws that would make it difficult or impossible for blacks to vote. The Fourteenth Amendment was not enough. The abolitionists were convinced that another amendment, a fifteenth, was needed that would fix the blacks' right to vote permanently in the Constitution of the United States.

There was vigorous opposition to such a proposal from Northern whites who did not want blacks to vote in their states. And there was equally vigorous support for a fifteenth amendment from Phillips and Sumner, and from Republican political leaders such as Stevens. The Republicans, who had a majority in Congress, wanted the votes of blacks in the North as well as in the South. The amendment passed in 1869. Though not all the northern states ratified it, the southern states that had not yet been readmitted to the Union were forced to do so. Their votes were enough, and in 1870 the Fifteenth Amendment became part of the Constitution. It did not say, as most abolitionists had hoped it would, that all men could vote. Instead, it said that the right to vote could not be denied to anyone because of his race or color or because he had once been a slave. The way was still open to keep the vote from those who owned no property or to those who could not read, and in this manner to bar most blacks from voting.

With the ratification of this amendment, most northern Republicans believed they had done enough for the former slaves. One constitutional amendment had freed them. Another had required the states to give them equal protection before the law. And now a third had required that black men be given the vote if they met all the other qualifications for voting in any state. From now on blacks, with the same legal rights as whites, could shift for themselves. The plea of the abolitionists to give each former slave family a plot of land and enough education to understand and protect its rights went unanswered.

What the more radical abolitionists had feared at the beginning of Reconstruction soon came to pass. By 1870 all the former Confederate states had been readmitted to the Union and now governed themselves. Federal troops were still stationed here and there in the South to put down violence, but the whites who had ruled those states before the war went quietly to work to regain their power. Votes were counted dishonestly, and the Ku Klux Klan, one of many white terrorist organizations, was formed to threaten, torture, and even murder blacks and any whites who tried to help blacks participate in government. Even without such measures, though, in most states whites were in the majority and could win elections. By 1877, when Reconstruction ended, the government of every southern state was back in the hands of former slaveholding Democrats and their friends.

At the time they did not dare to deny the vote to blacks outright. Until the end of the century blacks who were brave and persistent could still vote in the South, and many of them did. On rare occasions they could still elect a black to office. But the economic situation of the blacks was left almost as unendurable under what passed for freedom as it had been under slavery. Most blacks now worked as tenant farmers, or "sharecroppers" as they were called. They worked the white owner's land as before, and as before were given the use of a cabin, a mule, a plow, and tools, as well as seeds to plant. As slaves they had been given food, but now it was no longer free. Each pound of pork, each peck of cornmeal had to be paid for when the crop was sold. The same was true of clothes. The tenant farmer was entitled to half the crop, but he was lucky if at the end of the year his share could meet his debts. Forced to work for another year to pay off last year's debt, with little to show for his labor but the food, clothing, and cabin he would have had as a slave, and without even the protection in illness and old age that slavery might have given him, many blacks thought that freedom had brought them little indeed.

XII

EPILOGUE: The ABOLITIONIST LEGACY

WHAT can we say today of these zealots, these men and women, all now nearly a century dead, who devoted their lives to freedom and equality for blacks? In their own time they were resented, often hated, by most white Americans, even by those who disliked slavery. The abolitionists, who relentlessly forced the issue of slavery on Americans, and whom nothing could silence, were seen as fanatics and troublemakers. It was not only Southerners and slaveowners who feared and detested them. The mobs that broke up abolitionist meetings, burned Pennsylvania Hall, threatened Garrison's life, and killed Lovejoy were made up of Northerners, and many of their members were leading citizens in their communities. Americans wanted to forget slavery and think only of the West to be opened, the fortunes to be made, the golden future that lay ahead for their country.

In a way, it is hard to see what the abolitionists achieved. After Garrison had roared forth his attacks in *The Liberator* for thirty years, slavery seemed more firmly fixed than ever in American life. The domain of slavery extended across the South all the way through Texas, and all the western territories were now open to it. The slave codes of the individual states had been made much more rigid. The pursuers of escaped slaves had the power of the federal government behind them and could reach into every northern village. The judgments of the Supreme Court supported slavery. Thirty years of petitioning Congress had achieved nothing.

The efforts of the abolitionists to enter politics as an organized party seemed a total failure. All they did was split the vote and elect to the presidency the southern slaveholders, Polk and Taylor.

When the end of slavery finally came, it was not because the abolitionists had converted the American people to the cause of freedom for blacks. It came because the needs of fighting the Civil War made it inevitable. And the war was fought not to end slavery, but to save the Union.

After the war, the abolitionists won partial victories in gaining the passage of the Fourteenth and Fifteenth Amendments, which were supposed to guarantee to blacks the equal protection of the law and the right to vote. But even these victories came primarily because the Republicans needed black votes to stay in power, not because the American people had been converted to the abolitionists' views about the rights of blacks. The abolitionists never succeeded in winning support for black education or for effective measures to protect blacks from poverty and hunger or to give them jobs or land.

After 1875 the northern Republicans lost interest in the freedmen and left to the blacks themselves the burden of maintaining their rights. Another Civil Rights Act that would have made segregation illegal had been passed at the very end of the Reconstruction period, but in 1883 the Supreme Court declared it unconstitutional. And in 1896 the Court held that the Fourteenth Amendment could not keep the states from setting up separate schools or railroad cars or other accommodations for blacks so long as the separate facilities were "equal." Everyone knew that the schools and restaurants and hotels and cars that blacks were forced to use were not in fact equal, but that is how the law would stand for more than half a century.

As the nineteenth century ended blacks throughout the South were even more segregated than they had been under slavery. Despite what the Constitution said, they had lost the right to vote. They had been pushed out of most of the skilled jobs they had once had. Educational opportunities were few. To earn a living at all, most southern blacks had to work as sharecroppers, earning little more than they would have received as slaves. The Constitution said they were entitled to the equal protection of the law. But there were no black policemen or sheriffs or judges and almost no black lawyers. No blacks served on juries. Southern courthouses existed for the control or suppression of blacks, not for their protection.

And then there were the lynch mobs. Every year, hundreds of blacks were lynched—seized by mobs and hanged or shot or burned to death without trial, in punishment for crimes they may or may not have committed, or even for being, in white eyes, arrogant or insolent.

Of the gains won by and for blacks during the Civil War and Reconstruction, almost all except the bare end of slavery had been lost twenty-five years later. Why was this so? One reason was that the country ignored the warning of the more radical abolitionists that the end of slavery would mean little for southern blacks unless they had the land and education to maintain real freedom.

Also, the abolitionists had generated some opposition to slavery, but had never succeeded in winning friendship and support for black *people*. The Republicans who had voted Lincoln into office wanted to do away with slavery, but like Lincoln himself in his earlier years, they would have been glad if the blacks themselves disappeared from the country, along with the slavery that had brought them. There was little interest in true black equality, North or South.

Another reason was that in the years from 1880 to 1914 poor, illiterate immigrants from Europe flooded the cities of the North. Northerners of old American stock, frightened of the strange newcomers, thought it necessary to keep them from voting, at least until their ways had become like those of other Americans. The Northerners began to understand and share the feelings southern whites, especially those with property, had about black equality. More and more northern Republicans began to think that the South should be left to responsible white Southerners who would deal with the black problem in their own way.

By 1900 even northern historians were writing about Reconstruction from the point of view of Southern whites, denouncing Radical Republicans and abolitionists as misguided if not evil men. After their brief time of glory during and immediately after the Civil War, abolitionists were once more regarded as unreasonable, extreme, and vindictive troublemakers who had played a bad and destructive role in American history.

It might all seem a failure. And yet the abolitionist legacy was not entirely dead. There was Moorefield Storey, eminent white Boston lawyer, president of the American Bar Association, who as a young man had been the secretary of Senator Charles Sumner. He still held Sumner's abolitionist principles. And Oswald Garrison Villard, a wealthy newspaperman, grandson of William Lloyd Garrison, who was ready to go on fighting for his grandfather's beliefs. And Mary White Ovington, also the descendant of abolitionists. There were still others: W. E. B. DuBois, black scholar and writer, and Joel Spingarn, wealthy literary critic and Columbia University professor; they were among the intellectual heirs of abolition.

In 1909 these leaders joined others to found the National Association for the Advancement of Colored People (NAACP). A new movement for the liberation of blacks was formed, rooted in the old abolitionism. There was a newspaper, *The Crisis*, edited by DuBois, which played the part of Garrison's *Liberator*. There were pamphlets and speakers and conventions as of old. But there was one difference. In the time before the Civil War the Constitution, as interpreted by the courts of that day, was solidly on the side of slavery. Now the Thirteenth, Fourteenth, and Fifteenth Amendments had put it on the side of freedom, if only the courts could be persuaded truly to enforce them. Some of the abolitionists of Garrison's time had denounced the Constitution as a "Covenant with Death." Their heirs in the twentieth century could sue in the courts for rights the Constitution guaranteed. In legal case after legal case over the years the NAACP won little victories.

But the Supreme Court still held that the Constitution did not forbid a state from requiring that blacks and whites be separated in public places, so long as their treatment was "equal." And the Court held that private individuals, organizations, and business firms were allowed to discriminate against blacks in almost any way they liked. Labor unions were free to exclude blacks, factories were free to refuse to hire them, restaurants and hotels free to refuse to serve them. As a result, the legal victories that NAACP was able to win in its first forty years hardly made a dent in the massive oppression suffered by most blacks in the United States. It was very much like the frustration the original abolition movement met before the Civil War.

World War II began to change things. Blacks were needed in the armed services and in war industries. Measures were taken to give more blacks the opportunity to become military officers and to prevent discrimination in war factories. Even more important, the United States was fighting against Adolf Hitler, whose Nazi party preached hatred of blacks as well as of Jews and other "non-Aryans." Many Americans became ashamed of the whole idea of racial prejudice. Presidents Franklin D. Roosevelt and Harry S. Truman gave a new recognition to the status and dignity of black citizens.

Then in 1954 came the great decision of the Supreme Court in *Brown* v. *The Board of Education.* The Court held that the segregation of blacks in separate schools was unequal treatment, no matter how good the black schools. This was followed by other court decisions declaring unconstitutional state and local laws requiring racial segregation or in any way treating blacks differently from whites.

But these court decisions did not enforce themselves. Nor did they control the actions of private organizations that discriminated against blacks. And the South resisted the *Brown* decision. Segregated schools continued to operate. Black parents who wanted their children to be admitted to white schools had to bring the local governments to court —an expensive ordeal. Unions and employers continued to exclude blacks. Racists were determined that everything would go on as before.

At this show of contempt for law and justice, blacks began at last to lose their patience. In Montgomery, Alabama, they refused to ride in buses in which they were forced to take back seats, and forced the local bus system to abandon segregation. Students in Greensboro, North Carolina, filled the seats of lunch counters and waited, day after day, until they were served. Blacks marched and demonstrated in the deep South, pressing local authorities to comply with the law. In 1963 an enormous outpouring of blacks and whites, estimated at more than three hundred thousand, gathered in Washington to hear Reverend Martin Luther King, Jr., speaking from the Lincoln Memorial, proclaim his dream of an America freed at last of the burdens of racial prejudice.

In the deep South the bitterest enemies of racial equality fought back with violence. Blacks were beaten, even killed; police dogs and electric cattle prods were used on black demonstrators; a bomb was exploded in a black church in Birmingham, Alabama, killing young girls at Sunday school.

This wave of violence reawoke the spirit that had characterized the old abolitionists. By the mid-1960s, thousands of men and women, black and white, rose to fight for equal rights. Many were young people, students and recent graduates of colleges throughout the country. They came to the South in the summers of 1963 and 1964. They marched with local blacks in demonstrations; faced the armed police and sheriff's posses who blocked their way; taught blacks what they needed to know to pass the tests for voting and went to the registration offices with them. Young lawyers came South to try to represent local blacks and to protect them from lawless acts by police and sheriffs. Clergymen of all faiths and nuns and lay leaders gave a religious fervor to what became known as the Civil Rights Movement.

Here were heirs of Garrison and Weld and Phillips, the true abolitionists of the twentieth century. Disregarding their safety, they committed their whole beings to the fight for equality. In the generation of abolitionist activity before the Civil War many had been beaten or threatened, but Elijah Lovejoy was the only abolitionist leader who had been killed. In the 1960s dozens of men and women gave their lives. Medgar Evers, a black leader in Mississippi, was ambushed and murdered. Lemuel Penn, a black lieutenant-colonel in the United States Army Reserve, was shot and killed returning home from training exercises. James Reeb, a young white Unitarian minister, was beaten to death in Selma, Alabama. Viola Liuzzi, a white Detroit housewife who had come to the South to join in demonstrations for equality, was shot and killed apparently because she had given a ride to a young black man who sat beside her as they drove through the night.

Perhaps the most cynical and brutal murder was of three young men—two white youths from the North, Michael Schwerner and Andrew Goodman, and a black youth from the South, James Chaney. They were driving in a pickup truck, weary from a day's work persuading black citizens to register as voters, when they were arrested in a little Mississippi town on a trumped-up traffic charge. They were held in jail for several hours, then released, only to be seized by a band of thugs as soon as they had driven out of the little courthouse town. Then they simply disappeared. Later, on a tip from an informant, the FBI discovered their three bodies buried deep in a new earthen dam that was being built nearby. All had been shot, and there was evidence that the young black man at least had been tortured before he was killed.

Southern courts refused to convict those arrested for these and similar murders, however convincing the evidence. Once more the cause of equality seemed to be defeated. But now the whole nation was aroused. After President John F. Kennedy was assassinated in November 1963, following a summer of racial violence, Congress was moved at last to pass, over the next few years, a really effective series of civil rights bills. Segregation in restaurants, hotels, and other public places was made illegal, as was most segregation in housing. In states or parts of states in which blacks had found it difficult or impossible to register and vote, federal officials were sent in to register them and to supervise elections. The use of literacy tests and other indirect means of denying the vote to blacks was outlawed. Billions of dollars were poured into improving schools in poor, predominantly black school districts, into job training, and into other aspects of a war on poverty.

The days of violence were not ended. In March 1968, Martin Luther King, Jr., was assassinated. He was the most eloquent of the leaders for human rights and black equality. He was respected and admired by millions of whites, and was revered by blacks. His killing touched off a wave of rioting and arson in ghettoes in many cities and of despair among all friends of freedom, black and white. A few weeks later came the assassination of Robert F. Kennedy. Though racial factors were not involved in his killing, it removed one of the strongest white fighters for black rights, a man who was campaigning for the presidency and might have achieved in that office the power to bring about major changes in race relations.

These two senseless murders coming so close together, with the riots and disorders that accompanied them, sobered responsible men and women of all races and parties. Violence subsided; and except for occasional local disturbances over school bussing or residential integration, the movement for black rights has proceeded through legislatures, courts, and public persuasion.

Progress since that date has been uneven. Under President Nixon's administration a period of "benign neglect" of race problems began. Lacking determined national efforts to push the drive toward complete equality, the progress began to lag, and many battles have not yet been won. Segregated housing remains common in the United States, especially in larger northern cities, and segregated neighborhood schools follow the housing pattern. Even where equal opportunities are now offered, burdens of past discrimination often make it difficult for blacks to take advantage of them. Lack of educational opportunity in the past is a handicap today in competing for jobs. The average income of black families is still not much more than half that of whites. The burdens of poverty and unemployment rest far, far more heavily on blacks than they do on whites.

But if there is much to do, much has been done. Blacks do find education and employment increasingly open. The courts are responsive to their rights. Black mayors head many cities and blacks fill seats in Congress and in state legislatures in increasing numbers. Segregation in public accommodations is substantially ended. Almost no public figure, even in the deepest South, would today openly defend racism. For the first time in our history we can really and truly say that we are a nation dedicated to the proposition that all people are created equal, however far we may be from achieving that goal.

And it is the heritage of the abolitionists of old that we have to thank for what we have so far achieved. They may have been impractical men and women, all zeal and anger and little prudence or common sense. They may have been failures in their own day, sometimes losing what they might have won because they doggedly refused to compromise their ideals to win half-victories.

But it was just because those ideals remained

uncompromised that they could finally begin to triumph. It is because Garrison and Weld and Phillips and Douglass and Mott and hundreds like them were willing to dedicate their lives to the belief that all men and women are truly equal and truly brothers and sisters that we could never completely erase that ideal from our conscience. It was nearly forgotten for a generation or two, but never completely. It slumbered, ready to burst into flame in the hearts of a new breed of abolitionists when the times again awoke it.

When Martin Luther King, Jr., proclaimed from the Lincoln Memorial the dream of America he held; when Lyndon Johnson, the first president elected from the South since the Civil War, pledged to a black audience at Howard University that "We shall overcome!" one could almost hear the echo of Lundy and Garrison and Weld and Douglass and all their colleagues crying from the distant past, "Amen!"

BIBLIOGRAPHY

Barnes, Gilbert, *The Anti-Slavery Impulse, 1830–1844,* New York, 1933, Peter Smith.

Bartlett, Irving, *Wendell Phillips: Brahmin Radical,* Boston, 1961, Greenwood.

Bontemps, Anna Wendell, *Free at Last* (a biography of Frederick Douglass), New York, 1971, Dodd.

Buckmaster, Henrietta, *Freedom Bound,* New York, 1965, Macmillan.

Dillon, Merton Lynn, *Benjamin Lundy and the Struggle for Negro Freedom,* Urbana, 1966, Univ. of Illinois.

Donald, David Herbert, *Charles Sumner and the Coming of the Civil War,* New York, 1960, Knopf.

———, *Charles Sumner and the Rights of Man,* New York, 1976, Knopf.

Douglass, Frederick, *Life and Times of Frederick Douglass,* reprint of 1892 edition. New York, 1966, Crowell.

Dumond, Dwight L., *Anti-Slavery: The Crusade for Freedom in America,* Ann Arbor, 1961, Norton.

Fauset, Arthur Huff, *Sojourner Truth: God's Faithful Pilgrim,* New York, 1971, Russell.

Filler, Louis, *The Crusade against Slavery, 1830–1860,* New York, 1960, Harper & Row.

Fladeland, Betty Lorraine, *James Gillespie Birney,* Boston, 1955, Greenwood.

Franklin, John Hope, *From Slavery to Freedom: A History of Negro Americans,* 3rd ed., New York, 1967, Knopf.

Gill, John, *Tide without Turning: Elijah P. Lovejoy and Freedom of the Press,* Boston, 1958, Stan King.

Hare, Lloyd Custer Mayhew, *The Greatest American Woman: Lucretia Mott,* Boston, 1937, Greenwood.

Klagsbrun, Francine, *Freedom Now! The Story of the Abolitionists,* Boston, 1972, Houghton Mifflin.

Lerner, Gerda, *The Grimké Sisters from South Carolina,* Boston, 1967.

Macy, Jesse, *The Anti-Slavery Crusade,* New Haven, 1919, Yale Univ. Press.

Merrill, Walter McIntosh, *Against Wind and Tide: A Biography of William Lloyd Garrison,* Cambridge, 1963, Harvard Univ. Press.

Pease, Jane H., *Bound with Them in Chains,* Westport, 1972, Greenwood.

Petry, Ann, *Harriet Tubman: Conductor on the Underground Railroad,* New York, 1955, Crowell.

Quarles, Benjamin, *Black Abolitionists,* New York, 1969, Oxford Univ. Press.

———, *Frederick Douglass,* Washington, 1948, Atheneum.

Schor, Joel, *Henry Highland Garnet,* Westport, 1977, Greenwood.

Sherwin, Oscar, *Prophet of Liberty,* New York, 1958, Greenwood.

Siebert, Wilbur, *The Underground Railroad from Slavery to Freedom,* New York, 1967, Russell.

Thomas, Benjamin Platt, *Theodore Weld: Crusader for Freedom,* New York, 1973, Octagon.

Thomas, John L., *The Liberator, William Lloyd Garrison,* Boston, 1963, Little, Brown.

Wyatt-Brown, Bertram, *Lewis Tappan and the Evangelical War against Slavery,* New York, 1971, Atheneum.

INDEX